CW00585441

Words
of Life

THE BIBLE DAY BY DAY

EASTER EDITION JANUARY–APRIL 2005

Hodder & Stoughton
LONDON SYDNEY AUCKLAND
AND THE SALVATION ARMY

Copyright © 2004 by The Salvation Army

First published in Great Britain in 2004

The right of The Salvation Army to be identified as the
Author of the Work has been asserted by them in accordance with the
Copyright, Designs and Patents Act 1988.

10 9 8 7 6 5 4 3 2 1

British Library Cataloguing in Publication Data
A record for this book is available from the British Library

ISBN 0 340 86251 3

Typeset in NorfretBQ–Regular by AvonDataSet Ltd,
Bidford on Avon, Warwickshire

Printed and bound in Great Britain by
Bookmarque Ltd, Croydon, Surrey

The paper and board used in this paperback are natural
recyclable products made from wood grown in sustainable forests.
The manufacturing processes conform to the environmental
regulations of the country of origin.

Hodder & Stoughton
A Division of Hodder Headline Ltd
338 Euston Road
London NW1 3BH
www.madaboutbooks.com

PARADOX

A fine line
spider–thread thin
links sorrow and celebration
darkness and light
loss and gain

Look over the shoulder of sadness
joy lurks in the wings
waiting to make its entrance

Tip weakness on its head
strength spills out
taking me by surprise

Peer into the darkness of a tomb
light blazes forth
banishing the shadows

Every farewell heralds an arrival
every ending a new beginning
every crisis an opportunity
for new growth, deeper roots

Dead leaves falling in autumn
make mulch for winter's bleakness
and shade from summer's heat

So help me
God of paradox and mystery
to embrace struggle and suffering
to wait patiently for their transforming
to search the shadows that settle round my heart
and find reflected there the radiance of your face

Barbara Sampson
New Zealand

CONTENTS

Major Barbara Sampson writes . . .

CONTENTS

MAJOR BARBARA SAMPSON WRITES...

'May he keep you as the apple of his eye and hide you in the shadow of his wings.' With these words of blessing a friend ends her regular letters to me. To be the apple of God's eye is to be looked upon with favour and delight. To hide in the shadow of God's wings is to be held in the place of safety and protection.

I find these two images strong, helpful and reassuring. They remind me of a time when I was facing medical treatment far from home. As I waited for an afternoon hospital appointment, I felt the overwhelming darkness of loneliness and fear. Would this medical problem signal the end of our missionary service? Would it be the end of a dream my husband and I had held for so long?

As I tried to pray in that dark place, God showed me the picture of a mother hen with her wing stretched out over her chicks. Suddenly I saw the darkness, not as the shadow of abandonment, but as the shadow of God's arm, drawing me near in protection, holding me close to himself. That new perspective made all the difference. I wrote:

> *One day you will thank me for this time*
> *You'll see it is not meant for harm*
> *The shadow gathered o'er your head*
> *Is the shadow of my arm.*

The medical problem did indeed signal the end of our missionary service. It did indeed send us home with what felt like a bagful of broken dreams. But, over the years since then, I have watched in amazement as God has fashioned new dreams out of those broken pieces.

I see shadows differently now. No matter how deep and dark they may be, I know they will never separate me from God's love, nor stop him working out his purposes for my life. I've learned that when I'm hiding in the shadow of his wings (Ps 17:8) and resting in the shadow of the Almighty (Ps 91:1), I need not fear walking in the shadow of the valley (Ps 23:4).

May it be so for you as well.

ABBREVIATIONS USED

AV	Authorised (King James) Version
Amplified Bible	*The Amplified Bible*, Zondervan, 1965
JBP	*The New Testament in Modern English*, J. B. Phillips, Geoffrey Bles, 1958
The Message	*The Message: The New Testament, Psalms and Proverbs*, Eugene H. Peterson, NavPress, 1993, 1994, 1995. Scripture taken from *The Message* copyright © by Eugene H. Peterson, 1993, 1994, 1995. Used by permission of NavPress Publishing Group.
NIV	New International Version
NRSV	New Revised Standard Version
RSV	Revised Standard Version
SASB	*The Song Book of The Salvation Army*, 1986

SATURDAY 1 JANUARY
A Word for a New Year

Philippians 3:7–14

'One thing I do: Forgetting what is behind and straining towards what is ahead, I press on towards the goal to win the prize for which God has called me heavenwards in Christ Jesus' (vv. 13,14, NIV).

Welcome to 2005! At this moment the year is as clean as a newly laid carpet, as smooth as a beach after high tide, as uncluttered as the pages of a new diary.

The Salvation Army has designated 2005 as the Year for Children and Youth. The United Nations has named it the International Year of Microcredit. On the Chinese calendar, this is the year of the Rooster. If you were to mark this year in your diary as the year of the . . . . , what would it be? Does 2005 have a particular theme or colour or flavour for you? What are your projects, tasks and goals for this year?

Finding answers to these questions, it seems to me, is a lot more satisfying than making New Year's resolutions. I long ago gave up that practice, out of failure and frustration with myself. Now I find it helpful to start a new year with a promise from God's word. After all, God already knows what this year will hold. My part is to stay close to him, attentive to what he says.

In Paul's letter to the Philippian Christians, he gives three guidelines for any new beginning.

First, leave the past behind you. The Lord is your Rearguard. If there are issues from the past that need attention, God will remind you of them. If there are things from the past that cannot be changed or healed, then leave them in God's hands.

Second, move towards the things before you. The Lord is your Shepherd. No matter how old you are in the faith, there are more experiences of God's love up ahead than you have already known.

Third, rest in the Lord within you. The Lord is your Life. Go forward into this year, confident of God's lavish love (*1 John 3:1*), guarding the deposit of the Holy Spirit within you (*2 Tim 1:14*) and keeping your eyes on Jesus (*Heb 12:2*). He is the One who stood at the beginning of your faith journey and who will bring you all the way to the finishing line.

1

SUNDAY 2 JANUARY
A Prayer for Help

Psalm 140

'O LORD, I say to you, "You are my God." Hear, O LORD,
my cry for mercy' (v. 6, NIV).

Psalm 140 is a prayer for all who suffer violence. It is a psalm for the victim of false accusation. It is a psalm for a youngster who is treated like a punching bag. It is a psalm for anyone in an abusive situation. It is a psalm for a battered wife, a betrayed husband, a child caught in the middle of a vicious custody dispute. Whatever the presenting situation was for the psalmist who first wrote these words, there are many – far too many – modern–day applications.

'Rescue me . . . Protect me . . . Keep me,' the psalmist prays. His description of his assailants is graphic and gruesome. They are evil, violent, wicked, proud slanderers. Their savage attacks are both physical and verbal. With tongues as sharp as a serpent's and lips smeared with poison, they curse and slander and spread vicious rumours about him. Like hunters trapping defenceless animals, they are out to trip him up and ensnare him.

He has no other place to hide, nowhere else to go but to God. There he knows he has a place of refuge and deliverance. There he knows he can find protection and shelter. From that safe place he looks out at his pursuers and prays that God will let them fall into their own traps. This is not pretty praying. It sounds angry and vengeful but, at its heart, his prayer is a plea for justice on behalf of all who suffer at the hands of others.

'I know . . .' he says. What do you know today? Do you know God's blessing, his safety and protection? Then reach out beyond your safe place, in prayer and with compassion, to those who suffer violence and abuse and who, as yet, do not know that God loves them.

Other refuge have I none,
Hangs my helpless soul on thee;
Leave, ah! leave me not alone,
Still support and comfort me.
All my trust on thee is stayed,
All my help from thee I bring;
Cover my defenceless head
With the shadow of thy wing.
Charles Wesley, SASB 737

JACOB – A STONE IN HIS SHOE
Introduction

New Zealand poet Joy Cowley writes:

> *Lord, I'd like to be a pilgrim. By that, I mean*
> *I want to be serious about the spiritual life,*
> *regular worship, daily prayer, some effort to become*
> *a nicer person to my family and neighbours,*
> *the kind of thing You've talked about*
> *for more than two thousand years.*
> *But Lord, I'm not sure I can do it. I've read*
> *about pilgrimage and it seems to me*
> *that You ask a lot of followers, a hard road*
> *and steep mountains that have to be climbed.*
> *That's okay for holy disciples, but me,*
> *Lord, I'm just your average tag-along.*
> *I've never been one for steep mountains.*
> *I know now that I would never make it.*
> *I'm wondering, is there a compromise,*
> *some kind of easy slope for beginners?*
> *What's that, Lord? Oh. I see.*
> *The problem is not the mountain.*
> *It's the pebble in my shoes.*

'Pilgrimage'[1]

If, as the saying goes, a person of privilege is born with a silver spoon in their mouth, then Jacob should have been born with the accompaniment of a whole canteen of silver. He was born, however, with what could more accurately be described as a stone in his shoe. That stone was a grabbing, grasping attitude that saw him stumble and struggle from the moment of his birth, all through his growing years and into maturity.

Let us follow the story of this man's life and watch the remarkable transformation that takes place as God turns a man with a stone in his shoe into one of the great patriarchs of Israel.

MONDAY 3 JANUARY

The Beginning

Genesis 25:19–21

'Isaac prayed to the LORD on behalf of his wife, because she
was barren. The LORD answered his prayer, and his wife
Rebekah became pregnant' (v. 21, NIV).

Jacob's story, like anyone's story, begins not with the man himself, but with those who came before him. Before Jacob came Isaac, his gentle-spirited father who, as a youngster, did not resist as his own father prepared to slaughter him and who, as an adult, gladly accepted the wife whom others chose for him. Before Isaac came the great patriarch Abraham, man of faith, obedience and righteousness, who stood like a giant kauri tree at the beginning of the story of the Jewish nation.

Upstream from Jacob, then, there flowed deep waters of blessing. God's promise to Abraham, to make his descendants as numerous as the stars in the night sky (*Gen 15:5*), was passed on to Isaac, then on to Jacob and his children. Jacob himself would eventually be known as one of the patriarchs of Israel, standing shoulder to shoulder with his father Isaac and his grandfather Abraham. But Jacob's great story did not have a great beginning.

Isaac, the account tells us, was forty years old when he married Rebekah. He was sixty years old when Rebekah gave birth to twin boys. That is, twenty years of barrenness, twenty years of silence, of shame and stigma. In the light of God's promise of abundant fruitfulness to Isaac's father Abraham, Rebekah's barrenness must have been a very heavy burden to carry.

Did she take courage from what she knew of her mother-in-law, who carried a similar burden and who laughed out loud when she was told, long past her child-bearing years, that she was to have a son (*Gen 18:11,12*)? Did Isaac question the guidance that his servant had received, that Rebekah was the right wife for his master, and the one to carry on the promised line (see *Gen 24*)?

'How long?' cried the psalmist (*Ps 13:1–2*). 'Will you forget me for ever?' Those words must surely have been Isaac and Rebekah's lament during those endless years of waiting. Maybe they are your lament today as well. Pray them out to God once more. Then stand back, take a long look, and see what he is doing.

TUESDAY 4 JANUARY
What's in a Name?

Genesis 25:22–26

'The LORD said to her, "Two nations are in your womb,
and two peoples from within you will be separated; one people
will be stronger than the other, and the older will serve the younger"'
(v. 23, NIV).

During her long and difficult pregnancy, Rebekah must have wondered if barrenness was perhaps a blessed state after all. The movements within her womb are far more than the wondrous first stirrings of new life. The narrator reports that the babies 'jostled' each other within her. The word has an ominous, competitive sound, like bargain hunters elbowing each other at a spring sale.

Rebekah inquires of the Lord as to what the jostling means. God's answer is very clear. The jostling signifies she is carrying twins and that there will be conflict between them, with the younger prevailing. The word Rebekah receives does not describe the babies themselves. It gives no instruction for their parenting. It does not suggest that the younger is better than the older or more favoured by God, nor that he should be treated any differently by his parents. The whole focus of the word is on the 'nations' and 'peoples' who will come from these two – that is, their descendants.

The babies are born, Esau first, closely followed by Jacob holding Esau's heel. Esau is given the name that may mean 'hairy' and he is also called Edom, meaning 'red'. Names in the ancient world often made statements about deity, but they sometimes also offered commentary on the circumstances surrounding one's birth. A creative name might do both, one directly and the other using wordplay.

This seems to be the case with Jacob. In Hebrew his name means 'May the God El protect'. At the centre of the Hebrew word are the root letters for the word 'heel'. Thus his name contains both a statement about deity and a comment on the circumstances of his birth. It is misleading to say that his parents named him 'heel', but rather that his name would make people think of 'heel'.

The story of Rebekah's difficult pregnancy and the unusual birth of her twins would no doubt be repeated to all who shared her joy at this sign of fruitfulness after long years of infertility.

5

WEDNESDAY 5 JANUARY

Deceiving and Despising

Genesis 25:27–34

'Then Jacob gave Esau some bread and some lentil stew.
He ate and drank, and then got up and left. So Esau despised
his birthright' (v. 34, NIV).

Although Esau and Jacob are twins, they seem to be poles apart in personality and in likes and dislikes. Esau is the outdoors type, a skilful hunter, a man of the open country. Jacob is a quiet (literally 'wholesome') man who is content to stay inside. As well as these differences, there is also the rather ominous detail of parental favouritism. 'Isaac, who had a taste for wild game, loved Esau, but Rebekah loved Jacob' (v. 28). Such information may sound like an innocent description of parental love but, when read in the light of subsequent happenings, it becomes an early hint of family dysfunction.

Conflict between the two sons breaks out one day when Jacob is preparing a stew. Esau the hunter turns up, presumably empty-handed, declaring that he is starving. He wants to 'gulp down' some of the delicious red stew that Jacob is cooking. Jacob is more than willing to provide food for Esau, but at a price. He responds swiftly. He knows what he wants and he goes after it. Has he been waiting for this moment for some time? Has

Rebekah told him of the divine promise given to her before the boys' birth, that the younger would be stronger than the older? Certainly, in this moment, he speaks from a position of strength as he bargains for his older brother's birthright.

Esau seems oblivious of what he is about to surrender. Having described himself as famished, he now declares he is about to die unless he gets some food. The immediate prospect of satisfying the physical hunger pangs in his stomach is more important to Esau than his inheritance rights as first-born, some time in the future. As the aroma of lentil stew fills his nostrils and makes his mouth water, Esau gives in to Jacob's insistence to 'swear to me', says the words and sits down to eat. In this way he 'despises' ('spurns' or 'treats with contempt') his birthright and so earns the reputation of being 'godless' (see *Heb 12:16*).

Jacob now has the birthright, but he still needs the blessing.

THURSDAY 6 JANUARY

Mothers, Beware!

Genesis 27:1–10

'Now, my son, listen carefully and do what I tell you' (v. 8, NIV).

This chapter records the third round of battle and manipulation between Jacob and Esau. The first was at birth, the second concerned the birthright, the third is over a blessing.

Isaac, now old and almost blind, summons Esau on his own so that he might give him his blessing. It is unusual for an elderly parent not to summon all his children together for such an occasion. This very fact heightens the unfolding drama. Isaac tells Esau to hunt some game and to prepare 'the kind of tasty food I like'. Isaac may be an old man with diminishing physical strength, but he still has a good appetite! When he brings the food, Isaac says, he will give Esau his blessing.

Like Sarah lurking and listening inside the tent as the messengers of God speak with Abraham (18:10), Rebekah overhears the conversation between father and first-born son. As Esau leaves with his bow and arrow, Rebekah swings into action. She tells Jacob what she has heard, reporting the conversation in direct speech to make it sound a truly accurate record. For some reason she identifies Isaac as 'your father' and not as 'my husband'. She calls Esau 'your brother' and not 'my son'.

Rebekah does not discuss the matter with Jacob, nor does she give her suggestion as to what he should do. She simply issues an order. Isaac conversed with Esau, but Rebekah commands Jacob. Her plan is for Jacob to copy his brother's physical features and for her to copy Esau's culinary skills. Her goal is that Isaac will give his blessing to Jacob and not to Esau.

Where did this mother come from? Has something sinister been growing within her for years? Has natural mother love become an in-appropriate kind of controlling love that has not allowed her child the freedom to grow up and become his own person? Is Rebekah re-membering the earlier revelation of God, that the older would serve the younger? Does she think she is helping God to fulfil his word?

Whatever is in her heart, Rebekah is manipulative and deceit-ful. Mothers everywhere, beware!

FRIDAY 7 JANUARY

Jacob's Deceit

Genesis 27:11–29

' "Are you really my son Esau?" he asked. "I am," he replied'
(v. 24, NIV).

Rebekah's plan sounds improbable to Jacob. After all, he has smooth skin, while his brother is hairy. When Isaac realises the trick that is being played, won't the pretence bring about a curse rather than a blessing? 'No worries,' says Rebekah. Esau's clothes and some goatskins will solve the hairy problem. 'And as for the curse,' she says, 'let that fall on me.' The benefits of the blessing will be Jacob's, while the punishments of any curse will be hers.

So Jacob goes. His concern is not how goat meat can possibly taste like venison, nor how goatskins can feel like human skin, but simply whether he will get into trouble for carrying out his mother's deceitful plan. He knows that such deceitfulness, if found out, will forever disqualify him from any kind of paternal blessing and inheritance.

Rebekah's way of operating is as smooth as Jacob's skin. She searches Esau's wardrobe, finds his best clothes and puts them on Jacob. She covers the exposed parts of Jacob's skin – his hands and neck – with goatskins. So dressed, he goes in to Isaac.

The old man is surprised at 'Esau's' prompt return. Jacob adds dishonesty to deceit, claiming that 'the LORD your God [note, not 'my'] gave me success'. To the old man, Jacob feels like Esau, smells like Esau, but sounds like Jacob. Three times Isaac expresses his doubt that this really is his first-born son but, as Jacob leans forward to kiss his father, it is the smell of Esau's clothing that finally convinces him. Jacob's kiss is not unlike another kiss of betrayal given on a dark night in Gethsemane (see *Mark 14:45*).

Isaac blesses his son with agricultural fertility, heaven's dew and earth's richness. He blesses him with political supremacy over nations and over his own brothers. Then he cements the blessing by declaring curses on those who curse him and blessings on those who bless him. Old man Isaac speaks greater truth than he realises.

To all of this, Jacob makes no response. He receives it and leaves quickly. He has to get out before Esau returns.

8

SATURDAY 8 JANUARY
Esau's Distress

Genesis 27:30–40

'Esau said, "Isn't he rightly named Jacob? He has deceived me these two times: He took my birthright, and now he's taken my blessing!" Then he asked, "Haven't you reserved any blessing for me?" ' (v. 36, NIV).

Esau earns a place in the book of Hebrews, not as an example of faith to be followed, but as an example of godlessness for trading his spiritual birthright for a single meal, thereby losing the blessing he should have inherited. 'He could bring about no change of mind, though he sought the blessing with tears' (*Heb 12:17*).

Tears indeed, floods of them, when Esau comes in from hunting and brings the tasty food he has prepared for his father. Jacob has scarcely left when Esau arrives. One slips out as the other steps in. One wonders what would have happened if they had met head-on, Esau carrying food, Jacob carrying Esau's blessing.

When Jacob's deceit becomes clear, Isaac is as distressed as his son, but there is nothing he can do about it. A blessing is a blessing is a blessing. Once spoken, it cannot be withdrawn. Once offered to one son, it cannot be withdrawn and offered to another. Isaac outlines the blessing he has given to Jacob. 'I've made him your master, and all

his brothers his servants, and lavished grain and wine on him. I've given it all away' (*v. 37, The Message*). There is nothing left for Esau to claim. But Esau weeps again and begs his father for a blessing. 'Do you have only one blessing, my father? Bless me too!' (*v. 38, NIV*).

Distressed, Isaac speaks words that sound more like a curse than a blessing. They are the opposite of what he has just spoken to Jacob. Esau will not enjoy the agricultural fertility that is coming to his brother. He will receive neither his father's blessing, nor heaven's dew, nor earth's fatness. What's more, Esau is condemned to living like a predator, that is, by war and plunder. But, at some time in the future, when Esau grows restless, 'when you can't take it any more' (*v. 40, The Message*), he will break loose and run free.

Isaac may be a blind old man, unable to tell which of his sons is really Esau, but he still has far-seeing prophetic insight.

SUNDAY 9 JANUARY
An Evening Prayer

Psalm 141

'My eyes are fixed on you, O Sovereign LORD; in you I take refuge – do not give me over to death' (v. 8, NIV).

From earliest Christian times, Psalm 141 has been used as an evening prayer because of its reference to the evening sacrifice (*v. 2*). Perhaps the psalmist has watched the priest in the temple offering sacrifices. He prays that God will find his evening prayer as acceptable as the priestly sacrifices.

The morning is a great time to pray as we look forward to the day. 'Lord, I need your help today for that task, that appointment, that meeting. I need wisdom to write that assignment, discernment for that decision, courage to face that person.' Morning prayer is as important for the Christian as checking the sea conditions and weather forecast is for a sailor preparing to set out from harbour.

While morning prayer looks forward, evening prayer looks back and reviews the day. 'Thank you, Lord, for being with me in that task, for the delight of that unexpected encounter, for your clear guidance in that discussion.' Evening prayer reviews the mistakes and failures of the day as well, not as condemnation, but as an opportunity for confession. 'For those careless words, for that quick judgment, for that unhelpful criticism, Lord, I ask your forgiveness.'

The psalmist knew, just as we know, that temptations to sin lie all about us all through the day, often in very appealing guises. David here calls them 'delicacies' (*v. 4*). They are like those delicious, bite-size nibbles passed around on platters at a birthday celebration. They are like advertisements on TV that make a new car, a new outfit, a new variety of coffee a 'must have'.

Surrounded by such tempting delicacies, the psalmist lifts his heart to God. Giving in to temptation, he knows, is the way to death. Seeking refuge in God, he has discovered, is the only way to life. This is his evening prayer. Tomorrow evening, he will no doubt pray it all over again.

Once again here I stand
asking you to lead me by the hand
into your presence, Lord, that holy place,
where I find strength in you.
                                    Mandy Carian

MONDAY 10 JANUARY
Anger and Escape

Genesis 27:41–45

'When your brother is no longer angry with you and forgets what you did to him, I'll send word for you to come back from there. Why should I lose both of you in one day?' (v. 45, NIV).

Not unsurprisingly, Esau holds a grudge against Jacob for his trickery. A dark spirit rests on him as he broods over the way he has been cheated of his father's blessing. He cannot see the wrong he himself did in giving away his birthright in the first place. All he can see is his brother's deceit. As Esau seethes with anger, it is not long before a murderous plan begins to take shape in his mind.

Esau is not like Cain, who acted in a fit of uncontrollable passion and killed his brother (*Gen 4:8*). He is more like Absalom, who planned his revenge against his half-brother Amnon for two years (*2 Sam 13:23*). Esau is enraged but not impulsive. He muses to himself, but somehow his plan takes words and is reported to his mother.

Rebekah's earlier advice to Jacob was bad (*Gen 27:8,13*), but this time there is sense in what she says. She tells Jacob to go and live 'for a while' with her brother Laban in far-off Haran. Esau will hunt game in the open country, but he will not hunt down Jacob in Paddan Aram. She also assures Jacob that time heals all hurts. The day will come when Esau's rage will settle and the blessing incident will be nothing more than a faded memory.

Little does she know that Jacob's 'for a while' stay with Laban will become twenty years. Yet a part of that, the seven years he serves out of love for Rachel, will seem like only a few days (*29:20*).

In persuading Jacob to leave promptly, Rebekah's final plea to him is, 'Why should I lose both of you in one day?' If Jacob stays, he will be murdered and Esau will be executed for slaying his brother. So Jacob leaves the family home, armed only with his father's blessing.

To reflect on
Memories, especially painful ones, die only slowly, if at all. 'In a while' can feel like forever. Are there long-ago memories that you are still waiting for God to heal? Bring them consciously before him in prayer today.

TUESDAY 11 JANUARY

Jacob Leaves

Genesis 27:46–28:9

'May God Almighty bless you and make you fruitful and increase your numbers until you become a community of peoples' (v. 3, NIV).

Rebekah's first plot is to get Esau's blessing away from Esau. For this, she takes advantage of Isaac's failing physical condition. Her second plot is to get Jacob away from Esau. For this, she plays on Isaac's sense of disgust with Esau's marriages to pagan women. Raising with her husband the matter of a wife for Jacob, she says, in effect, 'You surely don't want a third Hittite daughter-in-law, do you?'

Isaac needs no convincing. He summons Jacob and blesses him, with no comment about Jacob having already received a blessing that should have been his brother's. This time Isaac knows it is Jacob he is blessing. He forbids Jacob to marry a Canaanite woman and sends him to Paddan Aram, the area where Rebekah's father Bethuel and her brother Laban live. Isaac instructs Jacob to marry the daughter of Laban, that is, his cousin. Such an alliance will strengthen the family identity.

Having made his instructions clear, Isaac blesses Jacob with the blessing of Abraham. This is the only time Isaac mentions his father. The God of Abraham was with Isaac (26:24) and now the blessing of Abraham is to be with Jacob. Isaac recognises he is a link in the chain of blessing, passing it along to his son and his descendants.

So Jacob leaves. One wonders whether he slips out quietly in the dead of night. Is there an emotional scene as Rebekah says goodbye to her favourite son, unaware that she will never see him again?

It is only after Jacob has gone that Esau realises how distasteful his marriages with Hittite women have been to his parents. In an attempt to redeem himself and to please them, he marries a woman who is his cousin, the daughter of his paternal uncle Ishmael, the son of Abraham and Hagar. But we are not told that Isaac and Rebekah even notice.

Esau stands at the edge of his family with three wives but no birthright and only a limited blessing. Jacob, with both birthright and blessing in hand, heads off to Paddan Aram in search of a bride.

WEDNESDAY 12 JANUARY
Amazing Promises, Amazing Grace

Genesis 28:10–15

'I am with you and will watch over you wherever you go, and I will bring you back to this land. I will not leave you until I have done what I have promised you' (v. 15, NIV).

Jacob goes looking for a wife but, somewhere between Beersheba and Haran, he finds God. Or rather, God finds him. Reaching 'a certain place', which may mean no place in particular, he stops for the night. Lying on the ground, he uses a stone for a pillow and goes to sleep.

He dreams of a stairway stretching from earth up into the sky. Heavenly beings, 'the angels of God', ascend and descend the stairway. Standing nearby is God himself, who speaks to Jacob. Surprisingly, God does not rebuke Jacob for his behaviour towards his father and brother. Yet there may be an indirect censure. When God says he is 'the God of Isaac', does Jacob not squirm a little, realising that he is being spoken to by the God of the man he has deceived and of whom he has taken advantage? Jacob was able to trick Esau and deceive Isaac, but what will he do with God?

God reveals himself to Jacob as the God of his grandfather and the God of his father. He is the God of the first generation. He is the God of the second generation. Will he be the God of the third generation?

God promises Jacob land, innumerable descendants and spiritual blessings through both himself and his offspring. In spite of Jacob's tarnished story of deceit, and in spite of the fact that he has neither wife nor children, he is to be the carrier of God's blessing to the world.

The list of promises continues. 'I am with you and will watch over you ... I will bring you back ... I will not leave you ... I have promised.' God is the giver, Jacob merely the receiver of God's unconditional guarantee of involvement in, protection over and guiding of his life. Even before Jacob has left the land, God promises to bring him back.

My heart rises up and wants to ask, 'What makes Jacob worthy of these amazing promises?' Stated bluntly, he does not deserve such lavish, extravagant grace. But then, do you or I?

Check out 1 John 3:1.

THURSDAY 13 JANUARY
From Pillow to Pillar

Genesis 28:16–22

'Then Jacob made a vow, saying, "If God will be with me and
will watch over me on this journey I am taking and will give me food
to eat and clothes to wear so that I return safely to my father's house,
then the LORD will be my God" ' (vv. 20,21, NIV).

When Jacob wakens, he realises something momentous has happened. The ordinary place where he has slept for the night has been made sacred by a divine presence. He is both shocked and surprised.

Early in the morning he takes the stone that has been his pillow for the night and raises it as a pillar. Pouring oil on top, he names the place Bethel, meaning 'house of God'. He then makes a vow, declaring that if God will be with him and will watch over him on his journey, giving him food to eat and clothes to wear, and will bring him back to his father's house, then …

It would be easy to read these words as old-dog Jacob playing his usual tricks, bargaining and dealing, treating God as an equal. 'You do this, God, and I'll do that.' This could even be an ancient form of the foxhole prayer, often prayed in war zones, 'If you get me out of this alive, then I'll give you my life.'

But as we read deeper into the story, it seems indeed that this is a moment of transformation for Jacob. Until now the God of Abraham has been his father's God. When he stood before Isaac, waiting for Esau's blessing, Jacob referred to 'the LORD your God' (27:20). Now, as he stands before the pillar he has raised, he pledges that 'the LORD will be my God' (v. 21).

In the face of God's amazing, unmerited promises, Jacob knows he is utterly dependent upon the mercy of God to carry them out. He was able to manipulate his father and trick his brother, but there is no way he can deceive God. He begins his vow, speaking of God as 'he', but at the end, he addresses God directly. 'Of all that you give me I will give you a tenth.' This one sentence may be enough to confirm Jacob's sincerity. The man born with a stone in his shoe sets up a memorial stone, acknowledges God as the source of his provisions and now commits himself to tithing.

FRIDAY 14 JANUARY
Rolling Away the Stone

Genesis 29:1–14a

'When Jacob saw Rachel daughter of Laban, his mother's brother, and Laban's sheep, he went over and rolled the stone away from the mouth of the well and watered his uncle's sheep' (v. 10, NIV).

Jacob is a man with a trail of stones already marking his path. In these verses, a large stone at a well becomes a meeting place for him and his cousin Rachel. A well did not have protective walls, so a heavy stone placed over the top would prevent people or animals from stumbling into it, guard against contamination and also regulate the use of the well.

When Jacob learns from the shepherds that they know Laban, his uncle, he asks, 'Is he well?' This may simply be a polite inquiry about the state of Laban's health but, coming from a man who has only ever been interested in his own well-being, it expresses a significant change in Jacob's focus.

Jacob is concerned also for the sheep who, to his way of thinking, have been rounded up for the night far too early. His tone suggests that he thinks the shepherds are not working as hard or as long as they should be. 'Back to work,' he urges. But, they respond, they have to wait until all the sheep are gathered and then they will roll the stone away from the opening of the well and water the sheep.

It is hard not to read the following scene with modern eyes. Beautiful girl comes with sheep. Jacob rolls up sleeves, shows rippling muscles, single-handedly rolls away the huge stone. Girl sighs, shepherds gape, Jacob kisses girl then weeps tears of gratitude. He has come to the right place and met the right person. And they all live happily... no, not quite. Jacob introduces himself to Rachel who runs off to tell her father, who then hurries back to welcome his nephew, his sister's son.

The passage is full of movement and emotion. It provides a vivid illustration of God's promise to be with Jacob (28:15). Far from coincidence, this scene at the well is surely an example of God at work.

Nothing by chance, nothing by luck
nothing just happens to be
God is here in control
every stone he can roll
to work out his purpose for me.

SATURDAY 15 JANUARY
The Deceiver is Deceived

Genesis 29:14b–30

' "We don't do it that way in our country," said Laban. "We don't marry off the younger daughter before the older. Enjoy your week of honeymoon, and then we'll give you the other one also. But it will cost you another seven years of work" ' (vv. 26,27, *The Message*).

Jacob works a whole month for his uncle before Laban raises the matter of pay. Jacob, however, is not interested in monetary wages. What he really wants is to marry Rachel. 'Lovely in form, and beautiful', Rachel is Laban's younger daughter. Leah, her older sister, has gentle, tender eyes. She may be older, but her eyes are the beautiful eyes of a person who looks much younger.

Unlike his grandfather's servant who arrived in this same area earlier for the purpose of finding a wife for Isaac, but with ten camels and gifts (see *Gen 24*), Jacob has arrived empty-handed. He has nothing to pay the bride price, the dowry, so he pledges himself to work for Laban for seven years in return for Rachel. Laban's response, 'It is better that I give her to you than to some other man,' may be deliberately ambiguous. While Jacob assumes the 'her' is Rachel, Laban obviously has his older daughter in mind.

The seven years Jacob works for Laban pass quickly and seem like only a few days. At the end of the time, Jacob says, in effect, 'Now then! My wife.' This is more of a demand than a request for Laban to make good his part of the arrangement. No spoken response is reported from Laban, but he gathers the townspeople for a wedding feast. Afterwards, presumably under the cover of a bridal veil and in a darkened wedding chamber, Leah is brought to Jacob.

Only in the morning does he discover the identity of his new wife and realise he has been tricked. When Jacob questions his father-in-law, Laban coolly explains his deception. 'It is not our custom here ...' (*NIV*). Ever quick-thinking, Laban offers a solution. 'Finish this daughter's bridal week; then we will give you the younger one also, in return for another seven years of work' (*v. 27*).

Jacob, who once pretended to be his older brother, finds himself married to Leah who pretends to be her younger sister. The trickster has met his match in more ways than one! The deceiver has been deceived!

SUNDAY 16 JANUARY

Prayer from a Cave

Psalm 142

'Look to my right and see; no-one is concerned for me.
I have no refuge; no-one cares for my life' (v. 4, NIV).

Psalm 142 is a prayer from a cave, as the superscription notes. Fleeing for his life from King Saul, David has found refuge in a cave (see *1 Sam 22:1*). From that dark and comfortless place he cries out to God. He looks to the right, the place where a helper or defender would normally stand, but there is no one there. He can come to no other conclusion but that no one is concerned for him, no one cares about him. Perhaps he remembers another day when he spoke with confidence of the Lord who was always before him, constantly at his right hand (*Ps 16:8*).

He resorts to crying, that is, not weeping, but crying out to God. 'I cry aloud . . . I lift up my voice . . . I pour out my complaint . . . I tell my trouble' (*vv. 1,2*). The psalmist knows from the history of his people that the action of crying out will meet with a powerful response.

The children of Israel, in slavery in Egypt, cried out to God and he heard their cry (*Exod 2:23*). During the period of the judges, the people of Israel suffered at the hands of the Midianites until they cried out to God for help and he answered them (*Judg 6:6–8*). In Nehemiah's day Ezra reminded the people of how God had heard their cry and rescued them, time and time again (*Neh 9:28*).

In the absence of human help, the psalmist casts himself upon God. He has no refuge – but God is his refuge. No one cares – but God cares. No one hears his cry – but God hears.

Are you praying 'from a cave' today? Are you in a small, tight, difficult place where, it seems, no one stands with you, no one is concerned about you, no one cares? Prayer from a cave has no time to dress up in fancy phrases. It uses stark words like 'Help!' and 'Scared!' and 'Now!', and simply casts itself upon God's mercy and grace.

Someone cares, someone cares,
Someone knows your deepest need,
your burden shares.
John Gowans, SASB 238

MONDAY 17 JANUARY
Then God Remembered Rachel

Genesis 29:31–30:2, 22–24

'Then God remembered Rachel; he listened to her and
opened her womb' (v. 22, NIV).

The complex web of Jacob's story continues to be woven as he settles down to life with Laban's daughters, beautiful-eyed Leah and beauty queen Rachel. Family favouritism (25:28) now gives way to marital favouritism. Wrestling between two brothers (25:22) becomes wrestling between two sisters (30:8).

Leah, the unloved wife, produces Jacob's first four sons, giving them names that reflect both her anguish and her hope. One of these sons, Levi, will become the ancestor of the Aaronic priestly line. Another, Judah, will become the ancestor of David and his royal line, and eventually of Jesus, the Messiah.

Rachel, the loved wife, is barren. Leah expresses no covetousness for Rachel's beauty, but Rachel greatly covets Leah's fertility. She rails at Jacob, 'Give me children, or I'll die!' These are sorrowfully prophetic words. Childlessness would not be a terminal condition for Rachel, but childbearing will (see 35:16–19).

Taking matters into her own hands, Rachel gives her maid Bilhah to Jacob in the hope that Bilhah will produce surrogate children for Rachel. Jacob goes along with the plan and Bilhah becomes pregnant. It seems that everyone except Rachel is able to conceive. Blessing upon blessing, the children Jacob fathers are all male. In this patriarchal period, sons were considered to be of greater value than daughters. When Leah eventually has a daughter, she is given a name but no explanation of what her name means (30:21).

As the bitter battle is fought out between Rachel and Leah, God's promise to Abraham, that his offspring would be as many as the stars in the sky, takes flesh, one child after another for Jacob. Then, at the end of the account, 'God remembered Rachel'. This 're-membering' may be a literal putting back together again of Rachel. God listens and opens her womb. She becomes pregnant, gives birth to a son and names him Joseph.

For a moment, our hearts stand still. We know the amazing story of this son of Jacob. It seems that, even when barrenness and bitterness, wrestling and wailing, scheming and struggling all cry 'No!', God is yet able to say 'Yes!'

18

TUESDAY 18 JANUARY

Jacob Prospers

Genesis 30:25–43

'In this way the man grew exceedingly prosperous and came
to own large flocks, and maidservants and menservants,
and camels and donkeys' (v. 43, NIV).

Rachel's successful delivery of Joseph secures her position in her husband's family and signals to Jacob that it is time to head back to Canaan. He asks Laban for permission to leave and take his wives and children with him. Laban wants him to stay, admitting that he has grown rich and has been blessed because of Jacob. Jacob acknowledges this but again asks permission to leave and they negotiate a settlement.

Jacob requests no wages except the dark-coloured sheep and variegated goats from Laban's flocks. In the Mediterranean world, the sheep are normally white and the goats are black. Jacob is therefore requesting the irregular, abnormal and presumably lesser parts of Laban's flocks. Laban agrees to the deal, then, in typical style, quietly removes all the dark-coloured sheep and the variegated goats from his flocks. He puts them in the care of his own sons, three days' distance away. Jacob is left with only the white sheep and the black goats to look after and, Laban considers, they are unlikely to produce irregularly-coloured offspring.

But old-dog Laban has not counted on young-pup Jacob's clever selective breeding techniques. Jacob knows a way to get white sheep and black goats to produce variegated young. He takes shoots of various trees, peels them in such a way that there are white (in Hebrew *laban*) stripes on them and places these in the watering troughs. When the animals come to drink, they mate and produce streaked or speckled or spotted young.

From these young, Jacob does further selective breeding, with the result that he builds up very large and healthy flocks and becomes exceedingly prosperous. But this is a changed Jacob. No longer playing merely by his own wits or by deceit, he testifies that it is God who has given him success and made him wealthy (*31:10–13*).

In the Bethel incident, one of God's promises was that Jacob would spread out to the west, east, north and south (*28:14*). By way of wives and children, maidservants and menservants, goats and sheep, camels and donkeys, that promise to Jacob is now being dramatically fulfilled.

WEDNESDAY 19 JANUARY
A Call to Go Back

'I am the God of Bethel, where you anointed a pillar and where you made a vow to me. Now leave this land at once and go back to your native land' (v. 13, NIV).

Reports of Laban's sons' resentment against Jacob, a definite cooling in Laban's attitude and finally a clear word from God all come together to make Jacob determined to go back to his father. Out in the field, away from Laban's ears, he tells his wives what he has decided. Using deliberate contrast, he says, 'Your father's attitude ... is not what it was before, but the God of my father has been with me.'

He reminds them of his years of devoted service, which Laban has rewarded by cheating him at every turn. But God has overruled, preventing Laban from harming him and giving him success in the spectacular increase of his flocks. Jacob tells his wives of his dream and of God's clear call to go back to his native land.

Surprisingly, Leah and Rachel need no convincing. They are quite prepared to go with Jacob. They know how their father has treated them and consider that they themselves have been 'sold'. In early Israelite society, the bride price paid by the husband's family was supposed to be held in trust in case it was needed to provide for the wife

if she were widowed or abandoned.

Jacob, of course, paid no bride price, but gave fourteen years of service in return for his two wives. Laban should have set aside the equivalent of his wages for his daughters' benefit, but obviously did not do so. Thus they consider they have been 'sold' to Jacob. Their father's house offers them no economic security, so they have no reason to stay.

Jacob gathers his household and flocks, leaves no farewell note, and flees from Laban, just as he had earlier fled from Esau. Rachel, beautiful wife-turned-thief, takes her father's household gods with her. Just as deception and theft marked Jacob's departure from Canaan, deception and theft accompany his return. Going back means that God is fulfilling yet another promise given to Jacob at Bethel (28:15), but going back also means facing Esau, the brother he has cheated.

To reflect on
Does God call you back to something – or someone – today?

THURSDAY 20 JANUARY
Laban's Pursuit

Genesis 31:22–35

'On the third day Laban was told that Jacob had fled' (v. 22, NIV).

Three days later, Laban learns that Jacob and his household have gone. Gathering relatives and close neighbours, Laban sets off in pursuit. Enraged at Jacob's absconding, he may well plan to drag them all back again. He may want to deal once and for all with Jacob for this latest and greatest deception. But, before Laban has a chance to confront Jacob, he himself is confronted in a night-time dream by God, who tells him not to threaten Jacob with any harm. Even if Laban feels he has a legitimate grievance, he is not to prosecute Jacob or take legal action against him.

When he eventually catches up with Jacob, Laban accuses him of carrying off his daughters like captives. Laban does not refer to Leah and Rachel as 'your wives', but as 'my daughters'. He pictures himself as a victim of Jacob's deception and as a hurt but understanding father. He claims that, had he known of their impending departure, he would have given them a farewell party. This claim and his sorrow at being denied even the privilege of kissing his daughters and grandchildren goodbye, might well engender sympathy from his watching relatives.

Laban accuses Jacob of doing 'a foolish thing' and claims he has every right to do him harm. As the patriarch of the family he does indeed have that right. But a greater power than Laban has already spoken caution and, to his credit, Laban listens.

His second accusation, 'Why did you steal my gods?' although stated much more briefly, is perhaps even more important to Laban than the carrying off of his daughters. Laban has respected Jacob's God, but Jacob has not respected Laban's gods. Jacob defends himself for their departure, stating that he was afraid Laban would come and forcibly take his daughters away from Jacob. As to the charge of the theft of the gods, Jacob pleads ignorance and unwittingly puts Rachel in danger (v. 32). Laban searches, Rachel deceives her father, the matter remains unresolved.

To reflect on
In an incident full of secrets and lies, God remains majestically in control.

FRIDAY 21 JANUARY
Jacob's Defence

Genesis 31:36–42

'If the God of my father, the God of Abraham and the Fear of Isaac,
had not been with me, you would surely have sent me
away empty-handed' (v. 42, NIV).

Flushed with anger, Jacob addresses the question of the stolen gods and Laban's frantic and futile search. He roundly defends his own integrity. 'What is my crime? What sin have I committed?' As the distance between father-in-law and son-in-law grows, Jacob calls on 'your relatives and mine' to act like witnesses in a lawsuit, deciding who is guilty and who is innocent.

Jacob then reviews the last twenty years, declaring his own unblemished record. For all that time he has served Laban faithfully and has done nothing to harm or disadvantage his father-in-law. 'Your sheep have not miscarried,' he says, using the Hebrew word for ewes which is also the word for Rachel's name. That is, for twenty years he has cared for his Rachel and for all Laban's 'rachels'.

What is more, Jacob claims he has made restitution to Laban for any of his flocks that were attacked and ravaged by wild animals. He himself has carried the cost of any animals stolen by day or night. He has endured all kinds of extreme weather conditions during that time, from scorching daytime heat to chilling night-time cold. Sleep has fled from him, just as he has fled from Laban. The changeable weather he has put up with has been just like his changeable father-in-law who has changed his wages time and again. The 'few days' that Jacob served for Rachel (29:20) are now depicted as twenty long years of arduous toil.

Jacob's only constant during this time has been the unfailing presence of 'the God of my father, the God of Abraham and the Fear of Isaac'. If it had not been for God, declares Jacob, he would have ended up with nothing.

Jacob's cry is echoed by the psalmist. 'If God hadn't been for us when everyone went against us, we would have been swallowed alive . . . Swept away . . . lost our lives in the wild, raging water. Oh, blessed be GOD! He didn't go off and leave us' (Ps 124:2–6, The Message).

To reflect on
If it had not been for God, where would you be today?

SATURDAY 22 JANUARY
Laban's Parting Shot

Genesis 31:43–55

'It was also called Mizpah, because he said, "May the LORD keep watch between you and me when we are away from each other" ' (v. 49, NIV).

Laban responds to Jacob's emotion-packed review of the last twenty years as if he has not heard a word. He still believes he has ownership of his daughters, grandchildren and flocks. He suggests that he and Jacob make a covenant. For Laban, this is not a religious act so much as one final attempt to maintain some control over his family. Laban sees the covenant between them as having two parts – an oral agreement (v. 44) and a mound and pillar to stand as a lasting visible witness to the agreement (v. 52).

Jacob responds, not with words, but with actions. He sets up a pillar, then tells Laban's kinsmen to gather stones with which he makes a mound. Jacob, accustomed pillar-maker as he is, sees such a mound as a memorial marking the spot of God's goodness. Laban, however, sees the mound as some kind of platform on which God will stand to watch for any violation of the covenant.

Laban names the spot 'witness heap' in his Aramaic language and Jacob translates it into Hebrew. The narrator adds the name Mizpah, meaning 'watchtower'. The mound, Laban explains, is to remind Jacob that he is not to mistreat Laban's daughters, nor take additional wives. It is also to remind Jacob that he is not to do any harm to his father-in-law. Laban calls on Jacob's God to watch between them, like a guard on sentry duty who constantly watches for trouble and raises the alarm at the first sign. Laban has no doubt that Jacob is liable to break the covenant. God will have to keep him under close observation!

Jacob agrees, offers a sacrifice then shares a meal with the assembled relatives. In the morning Laban kisses his daughters and grandchildren (but not Jacob, unlike on their first meeting) and says goodbye. To the very end of their dealings there is tension between these two. The 'Mizpah benediction', far from being a blessing between Laban and Jacob as they part, is in fact the summary of their long and fraught relationship marked by deception, fear and suspicion.

SUNDAY 23 JANUARY
A Message of Unfailing Love

Psalm 143

'Let the morning bring me word of your unfailing love,
for I have put my trust in you' (v. 8, NIV).

The psalmist is once again in a deep, dark place. He paints a picture of his situation. He is pursued by his enemy, crushed to the ground. Someone's heel is grinding him into the mud. His world is blanketed by depression. He feels 'like those long dead', forgotten, abandoned, as if no one cares that he ever existed. No wonder his heart is dismayed, his spirit faint. This is the bleak picture of his world, painted in ever-deepening shades of grey.

Been there? Done that? Is this a picture of your world too? Then notice the process the psalmist uses to pick himself up out of the mud. He remembers, meditates, considers, spreads out his hands, his soul thirsts for God (vv. 5,6). His prayer is that God will do all the things God is so good at doing: 'Answer . . . do not hide . . . show . . . rescue . . . teach . . . lead . . . preserve . . . bring . . . silence my enemies . . . destroy all my foes.'

At the heart of the psalmist's cry is a wonderful word of trust. 'Let the morning bring me word of your unfailing love, for I have put my trust in you.' In my mind's eye, I see a picture behind this verse.

Imagine the psalmist, sleepless and burdened through the long hours of the night. The darkness around him is matched by the darkness within. Then, as the first beams of light signal the coming of a new day, he lifts his head. Far in the distance he sees a runner approaching. He stands and waits. Breathless and glistening with perspiration, the runner reaches him and holds out a piece of paper. 'Here,' he says, 'a message for you.' Opening it, the psalmist reads the words, 'Unfailing Love Again Today'.

Is this the message you need a messenger to bring you today? No matter what the sin, the defeat, the discouragement, the false accusation, the overwhelming task, the tragedy, the sorrow . . . No matter how deep the darkness, no matter how terrible the failure, God wraps his arms of unfailing love around you once again today.

MONDAY 24 JANUARY
Panic, Prayer and Presents

Genesis 32:1–21

'I am unworthy of all the kindness and faithfulness you have shown your servant. I had only my staff when I crossed this Jordan, but now I have become two groups' (v. 10, NIV).

Jacob's departure from home, twenty years earlier, had been marked by an angelic encounter (*28:12*). Now, as he heads back home, another angelic meeting assures him of God's presence.

Jacob decides it is best to notify Esau of his return. He sends messengers on ahead with a threefold report. First, that he has been staying with Laban for all these years. The implication is, 'I have not been hiding, avoiding you or sneaking around behind your back.' Second, that he has abundant flocks and servants. The implication is, 'I am coming with plenty. I have no intention of taking anything from you.' Third, his reason for sending word on ahead is to find favour with Esau. The implication is, 'Let's forget about the past and start over again.'

When the messengers return with an ambiguous answer, namely that Esau is on his way accompanied by four hundred men, Jacob is thrown into panic. Are Esau's intentions friendly? Is he coming in welcome or in war?

Desperate, Jacob resorts to prayer. He refers to God as the God of Abraham and Isaac. He does not yet name him as 'my God'. He sounds a little whiny as he reminds God of his promises (*v. 9*) but, with a sincerity seldom seen in Jacob, he acknowledges his own unworthiness and God's kindness and faithfulness (*v. 10*). He prays for deliverance for himself and his household.

Overnight Jacob hatches a scheme to ensure a welcome from Esau. He selects a vast number of animals and sends them towards his brother, herd by herd, with a space between each group. He reckons the five distinct groups of animals arriving in succession will slow Esau's progress and also wear down his military readiness for ambush or attack. He instructs his messengers that each time Esau inquires about Jacob's whereabouts he is to be reported as always 'coming behind'.

The gifts exhaust Jacob's reserves, yet he still feels vulnerable to Esau's attack. This is precisely where God wants him – feeling in need, with nowhere else to turn but to God. Now Jacob's real struggle begins.

TUESDAY 25 JANUARY

A New Name

Genesis 32:22–32

'Then the man said, "Your name will no longer be Jacob,
but Israel, because you have struggled with God and with men
and have overcome" ' (v. 28, NIV).

On the threshold of Canaan, Jacob crosses the Jabbok River by night and suddenly finds himself in a wrestling match with 'a man'. Wrestling, jostling, struggling have been the story of Jacob's life. First it was with Esau, then with Laban. Now, as he is about to discover, it is God with whom he wrestles.

In spite of his age, Jacob is strong and persistent. They wrestle together until daybreak, when the man strikes Jacob and dislocates his hip. Still Jacob refuses to give up and asks the man for his blessing. Perhaps with the dawning of daylight, the understanding also dawns on Jacob that this is no mere man he is fighting, but God himself. On another day he got Isaac's blessing by trickery, but this blessing he can get only by clinging.

The man responds by asking Jacob's name. 'Jacob,' he answers. Somehow the confession of his name, with all its connotations of deception, paves the way for a new name. The man tells him he is no longer to be called Jacob, the name with a stigma. His new name is Israel, most likely meaning 'God

will rule'. This new name is not given in response to Jacob's repentance, nor is it a guarantee of his complete transformation. What it highlights is Jacob's assertiveness, his ability to cling and persist in spite of his injury and his insistent desire for his opponent's blessing.

Jacob asks the man his name, and he gives not his name, but the blessing Jacob wants. Once more Jacob makes a memorial of a place by naming it. He calls it 'Peniel', that is, the face of God. In recognising that God has himself stood in front of him, Jacob is somehow reassured about his forthcoming meeting with Esau. So he heads into Canaan with a new name and a new limp. The new name will remind him of his new destiny. The new limp will remind him of his encounter with the living God.

To reflect on
How is it that, with God, one has to lose in order to win?

WEDNESDAY 26 JANUARY
The Moment We've All Been Waiting For

Genesis 33:1–20

'Esau ran to meet Jacob and embraced him; he threw his arms around his neck and kissed him. And they wept' (v. 4, NIV).

Having wrestled all night with one man, Jacob now faces the daunting prospect of meeting Esau and his four hundred men. He divides his family into three groups with maid-servants in front, then Leah, then Rachel. Jacob himself limps forward at their head. He is no longer 'coming behind' (32:18). In a gesture of submission, he bows down seven times as he approaches his brother. Jacob knows he is at Esau's mercy. What will his brother do?

The spotlight falls on Esau as he gathers up his robes and runs towards Jacob. He flings himself in embrace on Jacob's neck and the two weep together. This is the same picture as the father in Jesus' parable welcoming home his prodigal son, who expects punishment and rejection but finds instead forgiveness and grace.

Looking over Jacob's shoulder, Esau sees the group of women and children who accompany him, and asks who they are. Jacob summarises their story by introducing them simply as the expression of God's favour, 'the children God has graciously given'. Wordlessly, the women and children bow before Esau.

Jacob presses gifts upon his brother. Esau refuses at first, declaring that he himself has plenty, but at last he receives them. Jacob's stealing of his birthright and blessing have obviously not left Esau destitute. Esau offers Jacob the gift of his presence and that of his men, to accompany Jacob to their destination, but Jacob refuses. Esau calls him 'my brother'; Jacob calls Esau 'my lord'. Jacob speaks of God's favour and repeatedly asks that he might find favour in Esau's eyes.

As Esau leaves, heading back to Seir, Jacob diverts his company to Succoth and to the city of Shechem, perhaps to keep some distance from Esau. Here he buys a plot of land and sets up an altar, naming it *El Elohe Israel*. It is a testimony to the God who has been with him in all his journey and brought him back to his land, as promised all those years earlier at Bethel (28:20–22). Now, for the very first time, Jacob names God as his God.

THURSDAY 27 JANUARY
Back to Bethel

Genesis 35:1–15

'Then God said to Jacob, "Go up to Bethel and settle there,
and build an altar there to God, who appeared to you when
you were fleeing from your brother Esau" ' (v. 1, NIV).

Jacob's decision to settle in Shechem proves not to be a good one, for a sordid incident occurs there involving Dinah, the daughter of Leah. The name of God that ends chapter 33 and begins chapter 35 is not mentioned at all in the intervening chapter.

God then tells Jacob to return to Bethel, the place of their first encounter when Jacob was fleeing from Esau. Going back gives Jacob the opportunity to review the past and to renew the present. Before they leave, he urges his whole household to put away their foreign gods, to purify themselves and to change their clothes. As Jacob himself knows full well, new beginnings need both inner and outer expression.

As soon as all the symbols of idolatry have been buried, Jacob and his company set out. His return to Bethel, accompanied by wives, children, servants and flocks, contrasts greatly to his first visit, when he came alone as a fugitive from his brother. His fear at that time is matched now by a fear from God that surrounds the company like a wall, protecting them from any opposition. Arriving at Bethel, Jacob once more renames it, calling it *El Bethel*, that is, 'The God of the House of God'.

God, who has called him back to Bethel, appears, blesses him, confirms his new name and reminds him of the great and glorious promises that were earlier given to Abraham and Isaac. In confirming Jacob's new name, God reminds him that the old Jacob nature, like his household's foreign gods, must be buried. Jacob must put on all the implications of his new name, Israel. God tells him to be fruitful and increase in number. This is not an encouragement for more children in the present, but a promise that, in the future, a nation and a host of tribes coming from his descendants will fill the land.

Jacob, as is now his custom, memorialises this encounter by building an altar.

To reflect on
God called Jacob back to Bethel for review and renewal. What might God be calling you back to today?

FRIDAY 28 JANUARY
Jacob's Many Sons

Genesis 35:16–29

'As she was having great difficulty in childbirth, the midwife
said to her, "Don't be afraid, for you have another son" ' (v. 17, NIV).

Jacob's story nears its conclusion with the summary of his family and the death of his father Isaac. His last son to be born, somewhere between Bethel and Ephrath (an old name for Bethlehem), is given the name Ben-Oni, meaning 'son of my trouble', by his mother Rachel. Jacob, however, changes his name to Benjamin, meaning 'son of my right hand', signifying the place of protection and good fortune. From the start of his life, Benjamin has two things that mark him out from his brothers. He is the only child of Jacob to be born in Canaan and he is the only child to be named by his father.

But, as Jacob gains a son, he loses a wife. Rachel, who declared she would die if she had no children (30:1), dies as she gives birth to her second son. Rachel, the beautiful woman Jacob loved and laboured for, and who was always his favourite wife. Rachel, who had no difficulty in leaving her father's home and who stole and sat upon her father's household gods as she headed off for a new life with Jacob (31:35).

How will God carry out his promises of fruitfulness, tribes and kings (35:11) with Rachel dead? As a memorial to Rachel, Jacob raises a pillar over her grave. For the third time he commemorates an event or person, either glorious (28:18; 35:14) or tragic, as this one is, by raising a pillar.

There follows a list of Jacob's twelve sons. Once again there is no mention of Dinah, his one daughter. The list is not in chronological order, but rather gathered around the names of his sons' mothers, with Leah, his first wife, and her sons named first.

Benjamin, the last–born son, is listed with his brother Joseph. This young man will soon be described as the son whom Israel (Jacob) loved 'more than any of his other sons, because he had been born to him in his old age' (see 37:3–4). So the themes of favouritism and jealousy, deception and lies continue to weave a tangled web. But that's another story.

SATURDAY 29 JANUARY
A Heart of Flesh

Ezekiel 36:24–28

'I will give you a new heart and put a new spirit in you;
I will remove from you your heart of stone and give you
a heart of flesh' (v. 26, NIV).

A trail of stones runs through Jacob's story. From the pebble in his shoe at birth, to the stone he rolled away from the mouth of the well so that the shepherds could water their sheep, to the pillars he raised to mark the holy places where God appeared to him. With every stone memorial, Jacob learned a little more of the God of his father Isaac and his grandfather Abraham. With every pillar raised, he understood a little more of God's covenant promises and of his own part in the divine scheme of things.

Jacob, like so many of the Bible characters, was flawed, just like us. Deception, grabbing, manipulation were his tools of trade. But the ever-gracious God dealt patiently with him, stone by stone, until Jacob realised that the destiny he had been promised would not come about by his own scheming, but rather by surrender to God.

Years later, God spoke a promise through the prophet Ezekiel that he would remove the heart of stone from his people and transplant into them a heart of flesh. In reading Jacob's story, we see the step-by-step unfolding of such an operation. May a similar heart transformation happen in these days for you and me as well.

There are times when a heart of stone
would suit me just fine
I could watch gruesome images on TV
and not wince
I could read the story of a little girl
murdered
and not weep
I could walk through a suffering world
and not feel a thing
But I know the cost would be too great
a heart of stone would make me
less than human
living dead

God help me to be open to your transplanting
a heart of flesh to replace the heart of stone
and when the weight of feeling and tears and vulnerability
becomes too great
Help me to understand that this too is
a gift of your love.

SUNDAY 30 JANUARY
A Prayer Worth Repeating

Psalm 144

'Blessed are the people of whom this is true; blessed are the people whose God is the LORD' (v. 15, NIV).

If, on reading Psalm 144, you hear echoes of other psalms, you are hearing correctly. 'O LORD, what is man that you care for him?' (v. 3) takes us back to Psalm 8. Life as a fleeting shadow (v. 4) recalls the words of Psalm 39. The 'new song' (v. 9) echoes across the hills from Psalm 33 and Psalm 96. Much of the first eleven verses of this psalm seem to be a repetition of Psalm 18, with only minor variations. Statements in that psalm become petitions in this one. Even within the psalm itself there is repetition (see vv. 7,8). Within just a few verses, the psalmist repeats the very same prayer (v. 11).

Before we write this off as poor literature, consider your own way of praying. Do you have a fresh, brand spanking new prayer every time you come to God? Or do you find yourself praying much the same things over and over again, morning by morning, day after day? Prayer is like sunrise – to be experienced and enjoyed every day, no matter how well we experienced and enjoyed it yesterday. Prayer is like dusting – there is always more to do than there is time for. Prayer

is everyday food like bread or rice or potatoes – solid, satisfying, nourishing. Prayer is not like chocolate sundae ice-cream sprinkled with nuts and covered with thick raspberry sauce – a special treat on a special occasion.

While the first eleven verses of this psalm are echoes from other psalms, the last four verses are unique to this one. They contain pictures of blessing. In the psalmist's world, God's blessings were measured by the number and health of one's children, the full storage capacity of one's barns, the size and strength of one's flocks, as well as safety, freedom and peace.

What does blessing look like in your situation? Find a word or picture of blessing in this psalm and let it be your prayer to God today. Let the fact that someone else has prayed these same words before tell you it is a prayer worth repeating!

SUFFERING AND STRUGGLE

Introduction

Preparing to write a series on suffering and struggle for this edition of *Words of Life* made me feel like a hopeful tourist planning a world trip. Where to start? Where to stop? The area is huge and there will always be far more to see, to explore, to reflect on, than can be covered in just a short time.

The question of suffering is never far away. Every early morning news bulletin seems to tell of yet another terrible accident, suicide bombing or inexplicable act of violence. The haunting eyes of famine victims stare out at us from our evening TV screens. But suffering is not confined just to those distant places of unrest and conflict that we have come to look upon as war zones. Suffering affects our neighbours, our work colleagues, our friends, and at times comes crashing uninvited into our homes as well. At such moments, the question of suffering stops being an academic one ('Why is there suffering in the world?') and becomes a painfully personal one ('Why is this happening to me?').

What is the Christian believer to do with suffering? Is faith in a loving God not some kind of insurance policy against suffering? Is there any answer to the question 'Why?'?

Over these next few weeks we are going to look at some of the questions around suffering and struggle. Like a month–long world trip, this series will not cover everything. There will still be far more to explore. But, hopefully, it will be a starting point, a launching pad to a greater understanding of the God who loves us unfailingly and who comes especially near to us when we suffer.

MONDAY 31 JANUARY
The God Who Suffers

Hosea 11:1–11

'When Israel was a child, I loved him, and out of Egypt I called my son. But the more I called Israel, the further they went from me' (vv. 1,2, NIV).

When it comes to the topic of suffering, the best starting point is not, 'Why me?' but God himself. God is at the beginning of this and every other matter to do with our Christian journey. To look at the question of suffering from God–as–the–beginning puts the whole matter into perspective.

The Greeks and Romans said it was unthinkable that God should suffer, for God would have to have feelings, to be able to be upset or hurt or angered. 'Impossible!' they said. But the testimony of Scripture tells us otherwise.

Within six chapters of the first book of the Bible, we read the words, 'The LORD was grieved that he had made man on the earth, and his heart was filled with pain' (Gen 6:6). When Saul faltered and failed as king of Israel, the narrator reports that 'the LORD was grieved that he had made Saul king' (1 Sam 15:35).

The psalmist wrote of God being angered and aroused to jealousy when the children of Israel rebelled against him and did not remember his great redeeming acts (Ps 78:58).

In the book of Ezekiel, God reacts to the idolatry of his people by declaring, 'I will deal with them in anger; I will not look on them with pity or spare them. Although they shout in my ears, I will not listen to them' (Ezek 8:18).

One of the greatest love stories in Scripture, the book of Hosea, reveals the heart of God laid bare. It tells the painful story of love rejected, of goodness spurned, of forgiveness tested again and again. Like a husband who keeps on loving his wayward wife, God loved, called, taught, healed, led and lifted his people. But they turned away, burned incense to other gods and refused to repent.

These and other references tell us that God is not distant, remote or unfeeling (SASB 238). He is not too far above our lives to be engaged, not too holy to be touched by our sinfulness, not too great to be concerned for our petty needs. God suffers because he loves so much.

TUESDAY 1 FEBRUARY
God Suffers for His Children

Exodus 3:1–10

'The LORD said, "I have indeed seen the misery of my people in Egypt. I have heard them crying out because of their slave drivers, and I am concerned about their suffering. So I have come down to rescue them" ' (vv. 7,8, NIV).

What parents do not suffer when their children suffer, whether from bullying, acne or fickle friendships? How amazing, and how comforting, to know that God suffers over his children as well.

God spoke to Moses through a burning bush at Horeb, saying that he had seen the misery of the children of Israel in Egypt. He had heard their crying out because of their slave drivers. He said, 'I am concerned about their suffering.' God's compassion (literally 'suffering with') resulted in his saving action on behalf of his people. 'So I have come down to rescue them.'

Time and again, as the story of the chosen people of Israel unfolded, God saw, heard and was moved by the distress of his people. Usually it was a self-imposed distress that came about when they wandered away from God, rebelled against his clearly stated guidelines for living and found themselves in strife. Time and again they called out to God. Ever patient, ever loving, as the prophet Isaiah wrote, 'In all their distress he [God] too was distressed, and the angel of his presence saved them. In his love and mercy he redeemed them; he lifted them up and carried them all the days of old' (Isa 63:9).

Isaiah takes the image even further and describes God as a woman in childbirth, crying out, gasping, panting, bringing faith to birth, delivering salvation to his people (see Isa 42:14). A few chapters later, the prophet has God asking the incredible question, 'Can a mother forget the baby at her breast and have no compassion on the child she has borne? Though she may forget, I will not forget you!' (49:15). To make sure he could not forget, God says, 'See, I have engraved you on the palms of my hands' (v. 16).

Take a moment to look at the palms of your hands. In this day of tattoos and body piercing, can you imagine the pain of having something engraved into your palm? This is what God has done out of love for you. The engraving looks strangely like nail prints.

WEDNESDAY 2 FEBRUARY
Man of Sorrows

Isaiah 53:1–7

'He was despised and rejected by men, a man of sorrows, and familiar with suffering. Like one from whom men hide their faces he was despised, and we esteemed him not' (v. 3, NIV).

Hundreds of years before he was born, Jesus was given the name, 'Man of Sorrows'. To that name were added the labels, 'despised', 'rejected', 'smitten', 'afflicted', 'pierced', 'crushed', 'familiar with suffering'.

Man of sorrows! What a name
For the Son of God, who came
Ruined sinners to reclaim.

He was born to a poor couple a long way from their home who found shelter in a lean-to shed. While he was still a toddler, his family became refugees on the run from the king of the land who somehow saw this youngster as a threat. Throughout his lifetime he suffered rejection and opposition. Those who knew him best were slow to understand who he was or what he was on about. Even his own family, his brothers and sisters, did not appreciate him.

Bearing shame and scoffing rude,
In my place condemned he stood,
Sealed my pardon with his blood.

To his disciples he spoke about carrying a cross, and some of them watched as he himself was nailed to one. He was forced to drink a cup of suffering he did not want, but there was no other way. On him was laid the iniquity of the whole world.

Guilty, vile and helpless we,
Spotless Lamb of God was he;
Full atonement – can it be?

In the moment of his death, God, the One he called *Abba*, 'Daddy', turned his back. Human abandonment must have been terrible, but being abandoned by the One who had always loved him must have been overwhelming. The word 'excruciating', with *crux* – the cross – at the centre, perhaps describes this experience for Jesus.

Lifted up was he to die;
It is finished! was his cry.

His death, however, was not the end of the story. His once-and-for-all-time sacrifice dealt with our sin once and for all. Three days later, he rose from death and is now seated at the right hand of the Father in heaven where he prays for you and me.

Now in Heaven, exalted high;
Hallelujah! What a Saviour!

Philip Bliss, *SASB* 118

THURSDAY 3 FEBRUARY
If God Is Good, Why Do Bad Things Happen?

Job 1:6–12

'The LORD said to Satan, "Very well, then, everything he has is in your hands, but on the man himself do not lay a finger" ' (v. 12, NIV).

Some years ago, a flight from Chicago to Pittsburgh crashed, killing more than a hundred people. Pastor Thad Barnum spent days at the crash site alongside coroners and clean-up crews. One day a man working nearby said to him, 'Do me a favour. When you get up in your pulpit on Sunday morning, don't let God off the hook.'

When a tragedy occurs, questions of 'Why?' and 'What?' and 'Who's to blame?' rush to the surface. Everyone wants an answer, but no one wants an easy, glib, unthinking answer. For believers, the struggle often centres on God's goodness and his power. If God is good, why do bad things happen? If God is powerful, why does he not prevent bad things happening? The Scriptures tell us three things believers need to do at such times.

First, wrestle with God. Ask the hard questions. Give voice to the lament. Think of Job who wrestled with God, or Naomi who gave vent to her bitterness of spirit, yet still held on to her belief in God's sovereignty.

Second, rest in God's grace. God's power is displayed in creation. It is shown in miracles and demonstrated in the resurrection from the dead. Even when we do not understand how, we can be sure that God is weaving all things together for good (*Rom 8:28*).

Third, reach for God's perspective. At the start of the book of Job, a curtain in the heavens is drawn back a little and a conversation heard in which Satan is given permission to test Job. In her book *Affliction*, author Edith Schaeffer says that same conversation happens over every believer. God allows us to be tested but, at the same time, promises both to uphold us in the testing and to bring us through it (see *1 Cor 10:13*).

When I'm overwhelmed with sorrow
that I cannot understand
help me rest in your compassion
let me know you hold my hand.
When I'm lost in grief's confusion
and my whole world breaks apart
help me choose to trust your purpose
let me know you guard my heart.

FRIDAY 4 FEBRUARY

In Weakness Strength

2 Corinthians 12:7–10

'When I am weak, then I am strong' (v. 10, NIV).

Marva Dawn is a woman with multiple physical disabilities. She has life-threatening diabetes, a crippled leg, frequent foot sores, constant intestinal pain, blindness in one eye, a deaf ear, cancer and kidney deficiencies. You might expect such a person to wrap herself up in cotton wool and give all her energy to simply surviving. But Marva Dawn is an author, theologian and scholar with multiple academic degrees, many best-selling books to her name and a worldwide ministry of teaching and encouragement.

In her book *Joy in Our Weakness* she writes of a theology of weakness which has been formed from her study of Scripture and her own painful and persistent chronic illness. She says that, while the world celebrates success, strength, efficiency, usefulness, position and power, a theology of weakness reminds us that each of us is helpless and hopeless in our sin and desperately in need of God's grace. 'Only through total reliance upon that grace are we able to live as God's servants in the world,' she writes.

Marva Dawn reckons that those who accept their weaknesses and acknowledge their dependence can teach us best about the grace that invades all our lives. She says that, in her experience, some of the Christians who have best understood this have been disabled people or those with severe limitations.

The apostle Paul would agree with Marva Dawn. He longed for, prayed for, pleaded for release from his crippling physical disability that he described as a 'thorn in my flesh' (v. 7). But God said, 'My grace is sufficient for you ... my power is made perfect in weakness' (v. 9). When Paul finally heard that, he began to see his struggle in a different light. From pleading to be rid of it, he came to the place of delighting in the weakness that enabled the grace of God to shine through him.

This is the mystery God invites us to today. What is your weakness, your 'thorn in the flesh'? Placed into God's hands, it could become your strength.

SATURDAY 5 FEBRUARY
Only My Body Is Breathing

Psalm 6

'My soul is in anguish. How long, O LORD, how long?' (v. 3, NIV).

I am aware that only my body is breathing
Thump, Thump.
A rather mechanical sound
To move blood in rivers throughout my
*   physical form*
It has to be or I would be dead
Stone cold in my coffin, deep in the earth
I would be unaware of its warmth

So wrote a friend suffering from clinical depression. Depression, as the medical people tell us, has to do with the state of the neurotransmitters and synapses of the brain. In other words, it has a physical starting point. For those who suffer from depression, however, it feels more like a spiritual problem. 'Where are you, God? Why have you abandoned me?'

My soul sleeps unaware now of my desire
*   to win*
To meet life head on and breathe with
*   inspiration*
To create my own horizons and chase my
*   dreams*
To turn each failure into a moment of
*   grace*
A coma for the soul
Created by, I know not what
Unwelcome, uninvited, intrusive

A man suffering from depression wrote of his journey back to wholeness. Vital to his recovery was a friend who came alongside, walked with him, listened much, said little, accepted and identified with him. 'He unlocked the brakes of fear that had been holding me back.'

The full moon and the stars cannot wake
*   it*
The crashing waves challenge its beat no
*   more*
The song of the bird and the sunrise can't
*   move it*
The cry of the child goes unheard
The miracle of a rose unfolded means
*   nothing*
The wind moving a field of grass goes
*   unnoticed*

The psalms are a refuge for those who suffer. 'How long, O LORD, how long?' cries the psalmist. An answer is not immediate. His anguish is still real, but God hears his cry for mercy and accepts his prayer (v. 9).

SUNDAY 6 FEBRUARY

A Song of Praise

Psalm 145

'Great is the LORD and most worthy of praise; his greatness
no-one can fathom' (v. 3, NIV).

The book of Psalms begins with blessedness ('Blessed is the man') and ends with praise ('Praise the LORD'). In between is a long journey, a reflection of the journey of life, that winds its way through joy and sorrow, complaint and confession, prayer and petition. At Psalm 145 we enter the final stage of the journey.

Psalm 145 is the A to Z of praise. Each verse begins with a successive letter of the Hebrew alphabet. There is not a hint of lament here, no anguish at God's non-appearance, no complaint about his silence or seeming indifference. There are no requests, no deep questions, no gut-wrenching confessions of sin. Just pure praise.

The psalmist praises God for the greatness of his being. He praises God for his mighty acts, using phrases like 'glorious splendour', 'wonderful works', 'abundant goodness'. He praises God for his compassionate nature, shown not only to his covenant people, but abundantly to all humankind. He praises God for his kingdom, his divine sovereignty and rule that continues generation after generation. He

praises God for his faithfulness and grace that bring him near to all who call on him. He praises God for watching over all who love him and for dealing decisively with the wicked, those who deliberately turn away from God and his ways.

The psalmist ends as he begins, with a promise to praise God. He invites all people everywhere to join him in this exuberant, joyful task. The psalmist would say to us, 'Praise is one thing you can do on earth as well as in heaven, so you might as well start practising now!'

This is a psalm to read out beneath the echoing arches of a great cathedral. It is a psalm to sing out with a full heart and many hallelujahs. It is a psalm to live out day by day by day.

To reflect on

Augustine began his Confessions by quoting Psalm 145:3. He claimed that, because human beings are God's creation, we cannot find contentment apart from God. 'Our hearts find no peace until they rest in you,' he wrote.

MONDAY 7 FEBRUARY
Do You Want to Get Well?

John 5:1–9

'When Jesus saw him lying there and learned that he had been
in this condition for a long time, he asked him, "Do you
want to get well?" ' (v. 6, NIV).

Against a background of feasting and celebration (v. 1), Jesus meets a man whose life has had little celebration in it. He is one of a company of disabled people who spend their days at the Pool of Bethesda near the Sheep Gate in Jerusalem. This man, described simply as 'an invalid', may be the old man of the group. He has been lying here for thirty-eight years. Presumably someone takes him home at night and brings him back again in the morning, but this is his patch, his place of belonging, the spot where the grey half-light of his existence is lived out.

In that lifetime of thirty-eight years he must have seen a lot of people come and go. He must have had many conversations, taken part in many debates. Is healing possible? Is sickness a sin? Is God good? Whatever the man's physical or mental problem, it has obviously become a way of life. He has no way, no hope, maybe no desire to ever be any different.

When Jesus comes along, takes in the scene and learns that this man has been here for so long, he asks the invalid one question. It is direct, factual, to the point. 'Do you want to get well?' Somehow that question cuts to the very heart of the matter. Perhaps it is a question he has never asked himself, never considered. It is obviously easier to blame 'no one' or 'someone' (v. 7) for his lack of healing.

Jesus cuts through the blame-shifting, fixes the man with a stare and says, 'Get up! Pick up your mat and walk.' Translated, that means, 'Don't keep blaming others for your suffering. Do something for yourself. Make a break with the old patterns. Step out into healing!' Amazingly, it works. The man stands up! Picks up his mat! And walks!

There are times when such a direct, no-nonsense word is just what we need to hear. It cuts through the daze of addictions, the cushions of self-pity and the hang-ups of hopelessness. Is it the word you need to hear from God today?

TUESDAY 8 FEBRUARY
What Do You Want Me to Do for You?

Mark 10:46–52

' "What do you want me to do for you?" Jesus asked him.
The blind man said, "Rabbi, I want to see" ' (v. 51, NIV).

The story of Jesus' healing of Blind Bartimaeus and the story of the healing of the invalid, which we considered yesterday, have both similarities and differences. What the two men hold in common is a need, a sorrowful story of suffering and affliction.

Unlike the invalid by the pool, this man has a name. He is not just referred to as 'a blind man', but is Bartimaeus, that is, the son of Timaeus. He belongs to a family. He is part of a community.

Bartimaeus cannot see, but he is perceptive, his hearing is acute and he has a perfect sense of timing. What's more, he knows what he wants. He may be a prisoner in a world of darkness, but he knows of a way out. That way is a Person who is heading, at that moment, right in his direction.

Bartimaeus calls out, 'Jesus, Son of David, have mercy on me!' The people shush him and tell him to be quiet, which only makes him shout out all the louder, 'Son of David, have mercy on me!' Jesus stops and orders the blind man to be brought. At this point the on-lookers change their tune and urge him to come. Throwing aside his cloak, Bartimaeus jumps to his feet and approaches Jesus.

Notice Jesus' tone – gentle, in-quiring, as respectful of Bartimaeus as the blind man has been of him. 'What do you want me to do for you?' As for the man by the Pool of Bethesda, Jesus' question goes to the heart of the matter. He gives Bartimaeus options. Does he want to see, or are there blessings in blindness that he would rather hold on to?

For Bartimaeus, the choice is clear. If blindness holds blessings, he has already had them. Now he longs for the blessings of sight. So he asks and receives. This bold son of Timaeus has the best of both blessed worlds.

To reflect on
Helen Keller found blessings in blindness. She wrote, 'I thank God for my handicaps, for through them I have found myself, my work, and my God.'

41

WEDNESDAY 9 FEBRUARY
Suffering Calls Us Home

Luke 15:11–24

'I will set out and go back to my father and say to him: Father,
I have sinned against heaven and against you' (v. 18, NIV).

Author C. S. Lewis wrote, 'God whispers to us in our pleasures, speaks in our conscience, but shouts in our pains: it is his megaphone to rouse a deaf world.' There are times when God clearly uses suffering to draw us to himself. Notice how a nation or a community turns to prayer when tragedy strikes. People realise that all the resources that are usually enough when things are going well falter and fail in the face of adversity and calamity.

Would the prodigal son ever have headed back to his waiting father if he had not felt terrible hunger pangs in his stomach as he scratched for food among the pig slops?

A friend of mine told me how God got her attention when she suddenly became unwell. In spite of a 'religious' upbringing, for years she had lived ignoring God. But through her illness she found a new faith in God and a hope in heaven.

Another woman told a large audience about the many foster homes she had lived in up to the age of eight. Moving from place to place, she eventually came to a home and family where she was happy and felt loved. Everything seemed perfect. Then one day she ran home from school to find her little brown suitcase packed and waiting for her. As she spoke of her heartache at having to move yet again, everyone in the audience could see that little brown suitcase. Noticing people's tears, she said, 'Oh, don't feel sorry for me. You see, my experiences brought me to God.'

God, who knows the big picture of our lives, uses all kinds of ways to speak his love to us. He may use soft whispers or gentle nudges, or he may use something far more dramatic to get our attention and call us to himself. Would you or I ever have been thrown onto God's resources if we had not encountered something too difficult for us to handle?

To reflect on
Is God using pain or suffering in your life today to bring you (back) home to himself?

THURSDAY 10 FEBRUARY
Fulfilling His Purpose

Psalm 138

'Though I walk in the midst of trouble . . . The LORD will fulfil
his purpose for me' (vv. 7,8, NIV).

There are times when we know God answers prayer. We pray before going on a journey and we reach our destination safely. We pray for guidance and find a clear way forward. We ask for a loved one to be restored to health and their strength returns. Thank you, Lord, you are so faithful.

Then there are other times when it seems that God does not even hear our prayers. An accident happens, a decision we make proves disastrous, a loved one, far from getting better, seems to get worse. What is God doing in these moments? Is he playing games, strengthening our faith one moment, shattering it the next?

The book of Acts is full of both God's answers and his silence. Think of the Holy Spirit coming on the Day of Pentecost, the Cornelius story that heralds the beginning of the mission to the Gentiles, or Saul's amazing, dramatic conversion. These events were clear evidence of God's intervention. But there were also bad things that happened, such as the martyrdom of Stephen and the subsequent persecution of believers.

Paul wrote to the Corinthian believers, listing his troubles, hardships, distresses, beatings, imprisonments, riots, sleepless nights and hunger (2 Cor 6:4–5), the church disputes and quarrels he had to face, an agonising thorn in the flesh. Why did Paul have to suffer so much? As someone said, 'If that's how God treats his friends, it's no wonder he has so few of them!'

Part of the mystery of faith is that sometimes God answers and at other times he is silent. But he is never caught off guard. The death of Stephen and the scattering of believers led to the wide spread of the gospel. Paul's time in prison gave him uninterrupted opportunity to write letters which are now part of our Scriptures.

Suffering is never the end of the story. Our troubles do not mean that God has abandoned us. Even when bad things happen and we do not sense God near, we can be sure that he is still working out his purposes for our lives (see *Rom 8:28*).

43

FRIDAY 11 FEBRUARY
God's Answer to Suffering

Philippians 3:7–11

'I want to know Christ and the power of his resurrection
and the fellowship of sharing in his sufferings, becoming like
him in his death' (v. 10, NIV).

If someone has never suffered and yet preaches about the blessings of pain, the redemptive nature of suffering or the gift of affliction, they may well be booed out of town. But if someone speaks about suffering from an 'inside' perspective, their words are worth listening to.

The name of Joni Eareckson Tada would be unknown to most of us if she had not, first, had a diving accident that left her paralysed; second, met God in a deeper way through her experience; and third, dedicated herself to telling out the story of God's grace. Joni says, 'When life is rosy, we may slide by with knowing about Jesus, with imitating him and quoting him and speaking of him. But only in suffering will we *know* Jesus.'

This is exactly what the apostle Paul discovered. He learned things about God in suffering that he could not have learned any other way. At the beginning of Paul's faith experience, when he had been blinded by his encounter with the living Jesus, he received a visit from Ananias. God sent this man to anoint Paul (then called Saul) and to tell him that suffering would be an inevitable part of his calling to take the gospel to both Jews and Gentiles (*Acts 9:15,16*).

Later Paul wrote to the Christians at Philippi, telling about the fellowship of sharing in Christ's sufferings. If the apostle had placed an advertisement in the *Philippian Flyer*, inviting people to the inaugural meeting of the Fellowship of the Suffering, not many people might have turned up. Suffering is not something we usually run to embrace. For Paul, however, and for Joni Eareckson Tada and for countless others, their experience of suffering made all the difference between knowing factual things about Jesus and knowing him personally.

Joni discovered that God gave her no explanation or answers to her questions about suffering. But God gave her himself. 'God wrote the book on suffering,' she said, 'and he called it Jesus.'

'God allows suffering between him and us so that nothing will come between him and us.'

Joni Eareckson Tada

Shattered for Transformation

Job 16:1–14

'All was well with me, but he shattered me; he seized me by
the neck and crushed me' (v. 12, NIV).

One of the Hebrew words for pain is *parpar*, expressing the idea of moving convulsively, struggling, twitching, jerking, such as is found in Job's description of his pain. 'All was well with me, but he *shattered* me.' In modern Hebrew, this word for convulsions is also the word for butterfly.

If you have ever watched a monarch butterfly emerge from its chrysalis, you will understand the picture behind the word. Out of pain and struggle the caterpillar becomes a beautiful butterfly. As a caterpillar crawls along the ground, does it look up in longing anticipation at a butterfly flitting past and say, 'One day I'm going to be like that'? Does it accept the tight fit of the chrysalis, saying, 'This is good. This is part of the process'? Does it welcome the struggle that signals the beginning of the transformation?

'All was well with me,' says Job as he looks back to the beginning of his story. He had a wife, seven sons and three daughters, many servants and a huge number of animals (see *Job 1:2–3*). The numbers are significant. Seven sons are a sign of completeness and large flocks the evidence of great wealth. Job himself, in the words of God, is blameless and upright (*2:3*). He is a man of integrity and honour. But, in a moment, everything changes. His servants are slaughtered, his flocks destroyed, his children killed. Job himself is afflicted with painful sores all over his body. No wonder he says that God has 'shattered' him.

A woman whose minister husband died after a long illness wrote the story of her journey through grief to gradual recovery. She called it *Shattered and Restored*.

Another man whose teenage daughter was murdered found refuge in God. 'Father, I don't understand, but I trust you,' he prayed over and over again. Out of his own suffering he found compassion for his daughter's killer and a profound longing to make Christ known. He said, 'Sometimes God crushes a petal to bring out its essence.'

What is God shattering and transforming in your life in these days?

Determined to Praise

Psalm 146

'I will praise the LORD all my life; I will sing praise to my God as long as I live' (v. 2, NIV).

Psalm 146, the first of four Halle-lujah psalms that bring the book of Psalms to a close, begins with a statement of intent. The psalmist's determination to praise God is like a couple speaking out their wedding vows. 'In good times and in bad, in sickness and in health, in abundance and in poverty . . . I will love you.' Such a bold declaration is made even before it can be fully tested. This *agape* love has little to do with feelings and everything to do with commitment.

The psalmist commits himself to praising God all his life, as long as he lives. What makes him so confident is a particular perspective on the world. He is a wise old man who has seen things come and go, kings rise and fall, and he has come to certain conclusions about life. 'Do you want to know where to find help – real, solid, lasting, life-transforming help?' he asks. 'Then don't look to politicians or government agencies, businessmen or local legends. Such people may build empires and skyscrapers but, when all is said and done, they are human just like the rest of us.'

'The one sure place to go,' says the psalmist, 'is to God himself.' After all, he is the Maker of heaven and earth who not only created the universe but also gave instructions on how it should be maintained. He has all power at his disposal. He is the saving Lord of history. He meets the needs of the oppressed, the hungry, the prisoners, the blind, those bowed down with adversity, the resident aliens, the widows and the fatherless. In other words, every need of every person can be met in God who lives and reigns forever.

This psalm finds an echo in the ministry of Jesus. This saving, healing, salvaging work is what he came to do (see *Luke 1:53; 4:18,19*). This is the good news of the gospel.

Let it be preached today in the orphanages of South Africa, the prisons of Peru, the hospitals of India. Let it also be lived out right where you are.

MONDAY 14 FEBRUARY

Looking into the Darkness

John 20:11–18

'Mary stood outside the tomb crying. As she wept, she bent over to look into the tomb' (v. 11, NIV).

The morning air was cool, the dew heavy on the ground as Mary Magdalene made her way to the tomb where Jesus' body had been laid. Seeing the heavy stone rolled away from the entrance, she ran to tell Peter and John. Confused, excited, breathless, her words tumbled out. 'They have taken the Lord . . . we don't know where' (v. 2).

The men dropped what they were doing and ran to the tomb. John got there first and bent over to look in, but Peter, in typical style, barged straight in. The linen burial cloths that had enfolded the body of Jesus were still there, but the body was gone. Short on detail at this point, the Gospel writer simply says that the men saw and believed, then went back home.

But Mary stayed. She could have run off like the others. She could have chosen not to come in the first place. But she stayed, a new layer of grief now settling on her heart as she realised she could not offer her final respects to the One she loved. At the cross she had wept to see him die. Now her tears were for herself. As she wept, she bent over to look into the tomb. There she saw, not just burial cloths, but angels, white and radiant, sitting where Jesus' body had been.

Henri Nouwen writes in *The Inner Voice of Love* of the importance of facing the darkness of our pain. 'You must go into the place of your pain . . . [in order to] deprive it of its power over you. You must trust that your experience of emptiness is not the final experience, that beyond it is a place where you are being held in love.'[2]

Mary's actions of bending and looking tell something of her courage. Instead of trying to escape, Mary embraced her sadness. Instead of fleeing, she faced it. She could have chosen to be anywhere else, doing any other thing on that crisp morning. But she came, bent over, looked into her darkness and saw, not just angels, but Jesus himself.

TUESDAY 15 FEBRUARY
The Place of Growth

Isaiah 38:9–20

'What can I say? He has spoken to me, and he himself has done this.
I will walk humbly all my years because of this anguish of my soul'
(v. 15, NIV).

Where do we learn patience? Most often in situations where it would be more natural to be impatient. How do we develop kindness, gentleness or self-control? Most often through those experiences where it would be all too easy to be quite the opposite. Where do we grow faith with fibre and muscle? Usually in the difficult places where we have no other hope to cling to but God.

Some years ago I was amazed, when I charted the high and low points of my life, to discover that my most challenging and difficult times were also my most significant times of growth as a Christian. My lows, in fact, were God's highs.

Our suffering so often feels like a negative thing, a burden. Ask anyone who battles daily with chronic illness or disability. Like a thief, suffering steals our sense of fun and laughter. It saps our energy. Occasionally it steals life itself. Surely it is something to be avoided at all costs.

Hezekiah, king of Judah from 715–686 BC, was not unlike David in his faithfulness to God. He tore down the places of idol worship and called the people of Israel back to God (2 *Kings* 18:1–7). But there came a day when Hezekiah's world fell apart. He became ill and God told him he was going to die. Bewildered, shattered, afraid, all he could do was cry out to God. The words of his prayer, recorded in Isaiah 38, are in the lament and praise style of the Psalms.

God spoke to Hezekiah, giving him more years to live but, even more important, bringing him to a place of deeper trust. His experience of illness became the place of encounter with God. Later the king wrote, 'Surely it was for my benefit that I suffered such anguish' (v. 17).

Lush growth happens more often in the valley than on the high mountain peaks. The place from which we want to escape, as author Jane Grayshon writes in *A Pathway to Pain*[3], may be the very place where God is waiting to be found.

WEDNESDAY 16 FEBRUARY
Shaped by Suffering

Romans 5:1–5

'We also rejoice in our sufferings, because we know that suffering produces perseverance; perseverance, character; and character, hope' (vv. 3,4, NIV).

Author Gordon MacDonald tells of meeting a young South African man, an official in the African National Congress, whose words and character left an indelible impression on him. With both sadness and optimism, the young man spoke of his nation, the reversal of apartheid and the healing that his beloved country still longs for. With gentleness and gratitude he spoke of his Christian faith that had sustained him through years of suffering.

As they talked, Gordon MacDonald asked him where he had received his training, assuming that it would be at one of the world's top universities. The young man smiled and said quietly, 'I trained on Robben Island.'

Robben Island was the offshore prison camp where many South African leaders were sent during the years when the white-dominated government tried to suppress the opponents of apartheid. For more than twenty years, Nelson Mandela was imprisoned there. 'You were with Mandela?' asked Gordon MacDonald, incredulous.

'Yes, for five years. He was in the cell next to mine. The government tried to get rid of all the young black leaders, so they were swept up and dumped on Robben Island. But it worked in our favour, for there we got our education.' He spoke of the days of exhausting physical labour at the rock quarry. But in the evenings, he said, they sat together while the old men spoke of their histories, taught their tribal languages and shared their dreams for a free South Africa.

'Most important of all,' he said, 'Mandela taught us that you can never accomplish anything as long as you hate your enemy. Hate his politics, hate the evil behind the politics, but never hate the person. It takes your strength away. That's where I got my training,' he said. 'Five years on Robben Island taught me how to forgive.'

The apostle Paul wrote that suffering produces perseverance; perseverance, character; and character, hope. In this young South African man, Gordon MacDonald saw the priceless hope that years of suffering had produced.

To reflect on
'Suffering is the chisel God uses to shape our souls.'

J. I. Packer

THURSDAY 17 FEBRUARY
Lessons from a Waiting Room

2 Corinthians 1:3–7

'The Father of compassion and the God of all comfort . . . comforts
us in all our troubles, so that we can comfort those in any
trouble with the comfort we ourselves have received from God'
(vv. 3,4, NIV).

Waiting rooms can be dark and difficult places. Questions paper the walls. Uncertainties rest like cushions on the chairs. Loneliness hangs around like threadbare curtains. Other people come and go, but most keep their thoughts to themselves. This is not a place for cheery chatter.

God's word gives some clear guidelines as to what to do for someone in a waiting room. Paul says that when we have troubles, God comforts us so we can pass that same comfort on to others when they have troubles. This comfort is more than a pat on the shoulder and a 'There, there, you'll be all right'. The word 'comfort' means 'with strength', so to comfort someone is to give them strength to carry on.

The first rule for a waiting room, then, is to embrace our own suffering. God never wastes anything. This double-mileage God uses all the experiences we go through for our own growth, then uses them again to pass strength on to others.

A hospital chaplain whose adult son died said that he discovered his best training for ministry was his own grievous loss. 'No matter how much I had prepared to help other people, I had to walk through my own anguish. I had to weep and mourn myself.'

The second rule for helping someone in a waiting room is to be there. If you cannot be there in person, then imagine yourself just outside the door, waiting for the one who waits inside. Push a prayer through the keyhole. Slip a note under the door. 'I'm thinking of you as you wait for the test result . . . as you remember this anniversary . . . as you make a new normal out of life.'

For all their bad press, Job's friends did at least this one thing right. They came and sat with him in silence for seven days until Job felt able to speak (Job 2:11–13).

The third rule for a waiting room is to make no judgments. Think of how the woman at the well responded when Jesus listened to her, uncovered her loneliness and offered her hope.

FRIDAY 18 FEBRUARY

The Gift of Pain

Luke 17:11–19

'One of them, when he saw he was healed, came back,
praising God in a loud voice' (v. 15, NIV).

Mother Teresa was to the dying destitute of India what Dr Paul Brand was to its leprosy sufferers. His name is revered, his story told with a kind of holy hush.

Paul Brand, born to missionary parents in India, grew up with an awareness of God's fingerprints over all of creation. His father died when Paul was just a teenager but his mother lived until her mid-nineties, devoting her life to bringing physical and spiritual healing to the poor people in the remote region of the Kolli Malai mountains. Called 'Mother of the Hills', Paul's mother rescued hundreds of unwanted babies at birth, nursed, reared and educated them. From his parents, Paul learned that love can only be applied person-to-person.

As a young doctor, Paul discovered that leprosy does its damage by destroying nerve endings. Patients could easily damage themselves by taking hold of a hot saucepan or wearing tight shoes. With no pain signals to alert the patients, they could suffer burns without being aware of them or pressure sores could form, leading to infection. 'I thank God for pain,' said Paul Brand. 'I cannot think of a greater gift to give my leprosy patients.' Over the years he spent millions of dollars trying to create a pain system for his patients.

Because of the stigma of leprosy, Paul realised that even greater than the damage to hands and feet was the inner pain of rejection and isolation. His task was to work in partnership with his patients to restore their dignity. 'We are treating a person, not a disease,' he said.

Towards the end of his life, he told author Philip Yancey, 'As I look back over a lifetime of surgery, the host of friends who once were patients bring me more joy than wealth could ever bring. I first met them when they were suffering and afraid. As their doctor, I shared their pain . . . It's strange – those of us who involve ourselves in places where there is the most suffering look back in surprise to find that it was there that we discovered the reality of joy.'

SATURDAY 19 FEBRUARY
The Tears of God

Romans 8:31–39

'I am convinced that neither death nor life . . . nor anything else in all creation, will be able to separate us from the love of God that is in Christ Jesus our Lord' (vv. 38,39, NIV).

On Sunday 23 January 1983, the Revd Dr William Sloane Coffin, senior minister at Riverside Church, New York, began his sermon by saying: 'A week ago last Monday night, driving in a terrible storm, my son Alexander – who to his friends was a real day-brightener, and to his family "fair as a star when only one is shining in the sky" – my twenty-four-year-old Alexander, who enjoyed beating his old man at every game, beat his father to the grave. My one consolation lies in knowing that when the waves closed over Alex's car, God's heart was the first of all our hearts to break.'

Central to the gospel message is the fact that our Saviour, Jesus Christ, suffered death in order to bring us into life. 'For the joy set before him, [he] endured the cross' (*Heb 12:2*), entering fully into its anguish and pain. Because of Jesus' sufferings, we can hold on to one sure lifeline whenever we, as believers, find ourselves being led along the Way of Suffering. That one sure, indisputable fact is that God suffers with us.

Lisa Goertz was a Jewish woman who lost most of her family in the Nazi holocaust, including her mother, husband, brother, son and daughter. At one point, when sixteen members of her family had disappeared, she decided to end her own life. In her book, *I Stepped into Freedom*, she wrote:

'I walked out into the night, feeble with hunger, half crazy with fear and fatigue, and made my way down to the River Neisse. In a few hours all would be over, I told myself. What a relief! And there it happened. Across the dark river I saw the Cross and Jesus Christ on it. His face was not the face of a victor; it was the face of a fellow-sufferer, full of love and understanding and compassion. We gazed at each other, both of us Jews, and then the vision disappeared.' For Lisa Goertz this was the beginning of her road to faith and personal healing.

To reflect on
The tears of God give meaning to history.

52

SUNDAY 20 FEBRUARY

Great is the Lord

Psalm 147

'Great is our LORD and mighty in power; his understanding has no limit' (v. 5, NIV).

On first reading, Psalm 147 sounds like any other psalm of praise. But read it carefully and a pattern of praise emerges. The psalm begins and ends with praise (Hebrew *Hallelu Yah*) then divides easily into three sections, each one beginning with an imperative: 'Praise the LORD' (*v. 1*), 'Sing to the LORD' (*v. 7*), 'Extol the LORD' (*v. 12*). Each section of the psalm gives attention to both creation and salvation.

In the first section (*vv. 1–6*), God is the Star-Thrower who names the stars as he tosses them out into space. But he is also the healing, gathering God who stoops to serve and comfort his distressed people. He is indeed Majesty and Meekness, Sovereignty and Servant, Lord and Lowly One.

The second section (*vv. 7–11*) calls on God's people to 'Sing ... [and] make music'. Such a command recalls Miriam's song of thanksgiving after the crossing of the Red Sea. 'I will sing to the LORD, for he is highly exalted' (*Exod 15:1*). The reason for praise at that time was God's deliverance. The reason for praise here is God's provision. He covers the sky with clouds, lets rain fall on the earth and makes grass grow on the hills. These gifts were commonly considered as coming from Baal, the god of nature.

The third section (*Ps 147:12–20*) again speaks of God's power over nature. He spreads snow like wool, scatters frost like ashes, hurls down hail like pebbles. These phenomena are more than extreme weather conditions. They are signs of God's power and control. As far as the psalmist is concerned, God rules the world, so even the weather is a theological matter!

The beauty of Psalm 147 is its declaration that the God who throws the stars into space is the One who heals the broken-hearted. The power behind the universe has a personal face, turned towards us in steadfast love (*v. 11b*). This psalm is an expression of the incarnation – the personal, intimate, inextricably involved 'enfleshing' of God in his world.

May our eyes be opened to God's presence and power with us today.

MONDAY 21 FEBRUARY
Walking with the Wounded

Luke 10:29–37

'A Samaritan, as he travelled, came where the man was; and when he saw him, he took pity on him' (v. 33, NIV).

In the elephant family, when one elephant is sick or injured, the others draw near and caress it with their trunks. As the family moves along, they walk slowly so the injured one can keep up. If it cannot walk, they try to keep it on its feet. If it falls, they use their trunks to help it back up. At the first sign of attack, the strong, healthy adults surround the weak or injured one to protect it. The elephant family is a lesson from the world of nature of how the body of Christ should work when someone is wounded, either literally, or with those deep, unseen wounds of the spirit.

Jesus told the story of a wounded man in response to a lawyer's trick question, 'Who is my neighbour?'. By the end of the story, the neighbour is clearly the one who shows mercy to the injured man. Notice the powerful verbs of this story.

The first thing that happened was that the Good Samaritan saw the wounded man. Really saw him. Not just with the passing glimpse of the priest or Levite who came before him. It is all too easy for us to merely glimpse the wounded who live next door to us or who sit alongside us in church. Easy to write people off as 'unusual' or 'unfriendly' or 'weird' when, in fact, they are wounded. Easy enough to expect them to get over whatever is bothering them when, in reality, they are raw and bleeding inside.

The Good Samaritan not only saw, but he had compassion. 'His heart went out to him' (v. 33, *The Message*). And that compassion showed itself in the form of bandages, healing oil, reviving wine, transport, accommodation, ongoing attention, payment. Was it costly? Of course. Did it take time and effort? For sure. But that nameless Samaritan's compassion restored the wounded man and helped him continue his journey. Go and do the same, says Jesus at the end of the story. Let compassion be the gift you offer to those who are wounded – no matter who they are.

TUESDAY 22 FEBRUARY
Strong at the Broken Places

Psalm 34:15–22

'The LORD is close to the broken-hearted and saves those who are crushed in spirit' (v. 18, NIV).

David wrote this psalm out of his own brokenness. If being 'a man after God's own heart' meant that he knew only a life of victory on top of the mountain, he would never have been able to offer a word of comfort to those who stagger along in the valley. David could speak confidently about the God of the Broken-hearted, because he had been there, done that himself.

What gave me, at one stage of my life, the right to sit alongside parents of children facing heart surgery? The fact that my child was facing it too. What enabled a friend to minister to parents of terminally ill children? The fact that she had lost a son to leukaemia. What gives an officer colleague the winsome ability to share the gospel with alcoholics? The fact that, not so long ago, he himself was also down and out.

This is the ongoing redemption of God in action. When the 'Why?' and the 'How?' and the 'What for?' of suffering have been, at least partially, worked through, those very struggles often become the gifts that we pass on to others struggling in a similar way. As Ernest Hemingway wrote, 'Life breaks us all and afterwards many are strong at the broken places.'

A man wrote of his earlier years when his ministry seemed fruitless. He saw his task as helping people to grow spiritually, but confessed that he often spoke with judgment, condemnation and condescension. Then his own tidy world was shattered when he and his wife adopted a little three-year-old girl who had been badly neglected and emotionally damaged as a baby. No matter what they did, they could not mend her brokenness. In the process, they too became broken.

Gradually, as he began to share out of his own struggles, he found people responding, not just to him, but to the gospel message. 'The only thing that had changed,' he said, 'was that God had cracked open the clay pot of my life.' A broken heart, he discovered, was a greater gift than having all the right answers.

WEDNESDAY 23 FEBRUARY
The Long Silence

Hebrews 12:1–3

'Let us fix our eyes on Jesus, the author and perfecter of our faith, who for the joy set before him endured the cross, scorning its shame, and sat down at the right hand of the throne of God' (v. 2, NIV).

John Stott said, 'I could never believe in God if it were not for the Cross.' In his play *The Long Silence*, he wrote:

'At the end of time billions of people were scattered on a great plain before God's throne. Some people were talking angrily. "Can God judge us? How can he know about suffering?" snapped a young woman. She ripped open a sleeve to reveal a tattooed number from a Nazi concentration camp. "We endured terror, beatings, torture, death!" In another group, a black boy lowered his collar. "What about this?" he demanded, showing a rope burn. "I was lynched for no crime but being black."

'Far out across the plain there were hundreds of such groups. Each had a complaint against God for the evil and suffering he permitted in his world. How lucky God was to live in heaven where everything was sweet and easy, with no tears or worries, no hunger or hatred.

'Each group decided to send a delegation to God. They chose as their leaders those who had suffered the most – a Jew, a Negro, a person from Hiroshima, a badly deformed arthritic, a thalidomide child. Together they talked and formed their plan. They decided that, before God could be qualified to be their Judge, he must endure what they had endured.

'They declared that God should be sentenced to live on earth as a man. Let him be born a Jew. Let the legitimacy of his birth be doubted. Let his family turn against him, his friends betray him. Let him be falsely accused, tried and convicted. Let him be tortured, abandoned, then let him die in a most shameful way.

'As the leaders announced their verdict on God, a long silence fell upon the crowd. No one spoke. No one moved. Everyone knew that God had already served his sentence.'

To reflect on

'People say, "There cannot be a God of love, because if there were, and he looked upon the world, his heart would break." The Church points to the Cross and says, "It did break." '

William Temple

THURSDAY 24 FEBRUARY
Living in the Valley of the Shadow

Psalm 23

'Even though I walk through the valley of the shadow of death,
I will fear no evil, for you are with me; your rod and your staff,
they comfort me' (v. 4, NIV).

It takes only a quick reading of the morning paper to remind us that the whole world lives in the valley of the shadow. Yet another suicide bomber wreaks havoc on unsuspecting guests in an Istanbul hotel. The exposure of yet another tragic case of child abuse leaves a community reeling. Yet another lone doctor closes up his practice in a remote location of the country, simply because of the endless demands of paperwork and the long working hours.

What do you do when the path you are travelling suddenly veers off the highway of happiness and dips into a dark detour, overgrown with obstacles and shaded by sorrows?

Houda was a Lebanese Christian who had experienced the horrors of life in Beirut. When asked how she and her church survived, she replied, 'We simply rehearsed the faith and sang God's story.'

That is what the children of Israel, exiled in Babylon, learned to do. At first, they found singing impossible. 'How can we sing the songs of the LORD while in a foreign land?' they asked (Ps 137:4). But as they sat in the shade of the trees that grew alongside the canals of Babylon, they remembered the words of Psalm 1, that the one who delights in the Lord and who meditates on his law day and night is like a tree planted by streams of water. As they remembered, their songs of lament gradually turned once more to songs of praise.

This is what Psalm 23 invites us to do when we walk in dark and difficult places. Singing the songs of the faith and telling again God's story remind us that God, in Christ, is both the Shepherd and the suffering Saviour who journeys this way with us through despair to hope, through death to resurrection. They remind us that his rod and staff, symbols of God's presence and protection, are always with us. They remind us that one day the shadows will clear, the journey will come to an end and we will be welcomed into the house of the Lord, where we will live forever.

FRIDAY 25 FEBRUARY
Living in the 'Meanwhile'

Hebrews 10:32–39

'In just a very little while, "He who is coming will come and will not delay" ' (v. 37, NIV).

Some people refer to it as 'living in the gap'. Author Marva Dawn calls it 'living in the "meanwhile" ', that space of time between the resurrection of Jesus and his return. In other words, the period of history that you and I are living in now. In this 'meanwhile' time, we need to hold two contrasting facts in tension. One fact is that our lives will not always be characterised by success. The other fact is that eventually we will triumph because Christ reigns. As a song says, 'I've read the end of the book and we win!'

A study of Revelation makes it clear that God will both have and give the victory eventually, but the 'meanwhile' entails suffering. The apostle Peter, writing to Christians scattered through Asia Minor, acknowledged their sufferings, gave guidelines for living the Christian life in an alien world, and encouraged them by saying: 'The God of all grace, who called you to his eternal glory in Christ, after you have suffered a little while, will himself restore you and make you strong, firm and steadfast. To him be the power for ever and ever. Amen' (1 Pet 5:10,11).

When our 'little while' feels like forever; when 'not long' feels like far too long; when pain and suffering feel like an endless season, we need to remember they are only that – a season that will pass as surely as autumn turns to winter and winter to spring.

There is no denying the fact of evil in the world. But the good news of the gospel is that God will not let us be defeated at the hands of evil, sin or death. Through the resurrection of Jesus, God has triumphed over sin and is even now restoring the world to its original design and purpose. Though we may have to undergo intense suffering in this present 'meanwhile' time, yet we are heading for resurrection and joy. As Paul so wonderfully proclaims, death and the grave, sin and evil, sorrow and suffering have all lost their sting (see 1 Cor 15:55).

Hallelujah! Come, Lord Jesus!

SATURDAY 26 FEBRUARY
Our Living Hope

1 Peter 1:3–9

'These have come so that your faith – of greater worth than gold, which perishes even though refined by fire – may be proved genuine and may result in praise, glory and honour when Jesus Christ is revealed' (v. 7, NIV).

On a cold, bleak Friday we huddled together, a little group of us, in the foyer of the local crematorium. We sang and spoke our final farewells to a dear elderly friend who had been promoted to Glory (as we say in The Salvation Army). Then we placed our hands on her casket and said, 'See you in the morning.' This is the hope of the Christian. This world is not our final destination. This day is but the evening before the greatest of all mornings.

When Professor Alan Lewis of New College, Edinburgh, was dying of cancer, he spoke out against 'the desperate, phoney cheerfulness that hopes for the best in the face of doom, this crossing of fingers that we might just get by.' He wrote, 'Eternity is divine love's greatest gift, unimaginable gift, already ahead, secure and waiting for us.' Paul said the same thing when he wrote, 'No eye has seen, no ear has heard, no mind has conceived what God has prepared for those who love him' (1 Cor 2:9).

A Ugandan Christian who suffered terrible wounds when the bus he was travelling on was attacked by guerrillas wrote, 'God never promises us an easy time. Just a safe arrival.'

One day it will all make sense. One day we will see how suffering and struggle, loss and grief have shaped us and refined our faith. One day, the Scriptures declare, God will usher in 'a new heaven and a new earth, the home of righteousness' (2 Pet 3:13) where there will be no more death or mourning or pain, and every tear will be wiped away from every eye (see Rev 21:4). In that day, says author Philip Yancey, 'God's miracle of transforming Bad Friday into Easter Sunday will be enlarged to cosmic scale.'

'Let us not be overthrown at the final test . . . In sorrow we must go, but not in despair. Behold! We are not bound forever to the circles of the world, and beyond them is more than memory.'
Aragorn in The Return of the King
by J. R. R. Tolkien[4]

SUNDAY 27 FEBRUARY

Symphony of Praise

Psalm 148

'Let them praise the name of the LORD, for his name alone is exalted; his splendour is above the earth and the heavens' (v. 13, NIV).

Psalm 148 is a symphony of praise. The psalmist is the conductor. Using his voice as a baton, he calls the heavens and all angelic heavenly hosts to praise. He brings in the sun and moon, the stars and the waters above the sky. He signals the earth and its creatures to join in. Great sea creatures, wild animals and cattle, small creatures and flying birds all add their sounds of praise to the symphony. Inanimate objects such as lightning and hail, snow, clouds and stormy winds, mountains, hills, fruit trees and cedars all join their voice as well. Human voices are then drawn in. Kings, princes and rulers, young men and women, old men and children are all invited to sing.

This is an expansive, exuberant call to worship. The psalmist is not just being poetic. He is doing more than using great, majestic words. He is expressing his deep belief that the whole universe has a distinctive voice, a particular offering to make in the symphony of praise. Even more than 'everything that has breath' (Ps 150:6), the psalmist calls on everything that exists to praise God.

The psalm recalls Genesis 1 and the order in which God created the heavens and the earth. Last to be created, yet also the crown of creation, is humankind. The psalm also recalls Genesis 9 and the covenant established after the flood with Noah and his descendants and with 'every living creature' (*Gen 9:9–16*).

Having given out a cosmic invitation and drawn everything in heaven and on earth into the symphony, the psalmist gives his reason for such a celebration. Put simply – God the Saviour rules! Because he is in charge of the whole universe, God's praise is incomplete without the participation of every voice, human and non-human, in heaven and in earth and in all creation. Come, join the symphony. Lift your voice, your heart, your life in praise to God today!

Joy to the world! The Lord is come;
Let earth receive her King,
Let every heart prepare him room
And Heaven and nature sing.
                    Isaac Watts, SASB 84

JOHN 3:16 – THE WORLD'S GREATEST TEXT
Introduction

A man named Nicodemus and a night–time encounter provide the setting for this greatest of all Scripture texts.

Nicodemus was a prominent member of the Jewish ruling council. He was also an undercover believer, a secret disciple of Jesus. With honest questions, he sought out Jesus one dark night but was given more than he expected – a breathtaking glimpse into the heart of the gospel.

John 3:16 has been called the world's greatest text. Children learn it when they are young. Preachers handle it with holy, awe–filled hands. Scholars and authors have written volumes on it. Believers who have walked with God for years never quite get over the wonder of it.

It has probably brought more people to faith in Jesus Christ and entrance into the Kingdom of God than any other verse of Scripture. Ten key words – *God, loved, world, gave, Son, whoever, believes, perish, have, life* – make up what has been called 'the constellation of the Redeemer in the firmament of divine revelation'.

These ten words form naturally into five matching pairs. During this week we are going to look in depth at these five pairs of words. No matter how familiar the text is to you, may you catch again the wonder of a God who loved you so much that he gave the most precious gift he had so that you may find life.

MONDAY 28 FEBRUARY

God . . . Son

John 3:16

'For God so loved the world, that he gave his only begotten Son,
that whosoever believeth in him should not perish,
but have everlasting life' (v. 16, KJV).

The beginning of this text is God, just as the beginning of Genesis 1 is God and the beginning of Exodus 20 is God. Whether in creation, holy living or redemption, God is always the starting point. The creative work of God is summed up in ten declarations in Genesis 1 ('And God said . . .'). God's directions for holy living are given in ten commandments in Exodus 20 ('You shall . . . You shall not . . .'). The redemptive work of God is summed up in ten key words in John 3:16.

The word pair of 'God' and 'Son' expresses the giver and the gift, the author and finisher, the Alpha and Omega of salvation. God and his Son are two eternal, always-existing, uncreated members of the Godhead. God is described in Scripture as omniscient (all-knowing), omnipotent (all-powerful) and omnipresent (everywhere present).

God is the One who sits high and lifted up, worshipped by adoring angels, by cherubim and seraphim, and in whose presence they hide behind their wings and cry, 'Holy, holy, holy is the Lord Almighty' (Isa 6:3).

God, the Creator, Preserver and Governor of all things (*Doctrine 2 of The Salvation Army*), threw stars into space and starfish into the sea, created galaxies and orang-utans, moulded mountains and mankind. No word is too high, no description too great, no name too deep to tell who God is.

God is called Elohim, Jehovah, Adonai, the God who reveals himself by many names and who, in the person of his Son, reveals himself as incarnate love.

In the King James Version of John 3:16, the middle word is 'Son'. That is significant, for Jesus is central to salvation. God's plan for humankind, God's programme for his world, God's purpose in the universe, God's priority for time and eternity, all centre in Jesus. He is the 'heir of all things . . . the radiance of God's glory . . . the exact representation of his being' (*Heb 1:2,3*).

Read John 3:16 out loud with emphasis on the words 'God' and 'Son'. Let the richness of the text sink deep into your spirit today.

TUESDAY 1 MARCH
Loved . . . Gave

John 3:16

'For God loved the world so much that he gave his only Son,
so that everyone who believes in him should not be lost,
but should have eternal life' (v. 16, JBP).

In describing what God did for the world, the words 'loved' and 'gave' belong together. These are the God-verbs of this text. God's giving was the supernatural outcome of his loving.

God, ever the Initiator, the One who stands at the beginning of our salvation, loved and gave. Past tense – it happened. Past aorist tense, to use a Greek grammatical term – it happened once and for all. As the writer of the letter to the Hebrews says, Jesus is 'unlike the other high priests, [for] he does not need to offer sacrifices day after day, first for his own sins, and then for the sins of the people. He sacrificed for their sins once for all when he offered himself' (*Heb 7:27*).

We use the word 'love' to describe everything from a great movie to strawberry ice cream to days off work. Such overuse of the word has diluted its significance and wasted its muscle. God's love, in contrast, is stronger than death, the love that will not let us go, the love that many waters cannot quench, the love that suffers long and is kind, the love that never fails,

the love that passes knowledge, the love that rejoices in the truth, the love that always protects, always trusts, always hopes, always perseveres, the love that lasts for ever.

And this is how God showed his love. 'He sent his one and only Son into the world that we might live through him ... He loved us and sent his Son as an atoning sacrifice for our sins' (*1 John 4:9,10*). In his letter, John uses the word 'sent' to describe what God did. In his Gospel he uses the word 'gave'. The words are used interchangeably.

God will never take back his gift. He will never say, 'Oh, I didn't really mean you to keep it.' Jesus has been handed over to the world. He is God's forever gift of love to you and me.

Read John 3:16 out loud with emphasis on the words 'loved' and 'gave'. Let the richness of the text sink deep into your spirit today.

WEDNESDAY 2 MARCH
World . . . Whoever

John 3:16

'For God so loved the world that he gave his only Son,
that whoever believes in him should not perish but have eternal life'
(v. 16, RSV).

The word pair of 'world' and 'whoever' takes us from largeness to smallness, from macro to micro. God reached out arms of love to embrace the whole world, but his arms also envelop me.

The 'world' in this text is the Greek word *kosmos*. It does not refer to the natural world of trees, animals and plants. The 'world' is the realm of humanity that has gone its own way in rebellion against God. God gave Jesus to the world in his incarnation, knowing that sacrifice would be needed to redeem the world (see *1:29; 3:17*).

Jesus did not come into the world to save a select few, a chosen élite. Rather, he came to save the whole world, the all-encompassing circle of men and women who inhabit this planet, and who hide in darkness because of their sins (*v. 19*). Jesus died 'for the sins of the whole world' (*1 John 2:2*). In giving Jesus to the world, God has given him to all people universally, without distinction or exception. No one is excluded. All are welcome. This is the big picture of John 3:16.

The word 'whoever' means what it says. Every individual person is loved, welcomed and offered the gift of God's love as shown in Jesus. God loves the world one person at a time, as though that person were the only one in the world to love. To catch the impact of this truth, insert your name into the text. 'For God so loved . . . . that he gave his only Son, that if . . . . believes in him, ... will not perish but will have eternal life.'

This truth of the wide, all-embracing reach of God's love would be mind-blowing to the Jews. They believed they were God's specially chosen people, loved exclusively with a love that drew them in but closed others out. The truth is that God has no favourites, but everyone can say, 'I am the one Jesus loves!'

Read John 3:16 out loud with emphasis on the words 'world' and 'whoever'. Let the richness of the text sink deep into your spirit today.

THURSDAY 3 MARCH
Believe . . . Have

John 3:16

'For God so greatly loved and dearly prized the world that
He even gave up His only-begotten unique Son, so that whoever
believes in, trusts, clings to, relies on Him shall not perish –
come to destruction, be lost – but have eternal everlasting life'
(v. 16, *Amplified Bible*).

The words 'loved' and 'gave' are the God-verbs of this text. The words 'believe' and 'have' are the human verbs. These words express what you and I and 'whoever' need to do in order to make the truths of John 3:16 our own.

The verb 'believe' is one of John's favourite words, peppered throughout his Gospel. To believe is more than a casual response. ('Is it raining yet?' 'I believe so.') To believe is more than an intellectual response. ('They say Jesus is God.' 'I believe that is true.')

Belief is to the Christian what a life raft is to a passenger on the *Titanic*. To believe is to cast ourselves upon God's mercy and grace, to put our confidence in him, to trust that he alone can save us. To believe is to rest the weight of our load upon God's promises and to rely on him to carry out those promises. Belief is a matter of both the head and the heart. 'My head tells me I can trust God. My heart puts that trust into action.'

God will never barge his way into our hearts uninvited. He stands at the door and knocks (*Rev 3:20*). He longs to be gracious to us. He rises to show us compassion (*Isa 30:18*). But, like a gentleman, he waits for our response. He calls us to trust his Son today and for eternity. Our strong assurance is the promise that, 'He [Jesus] is able . . . to save to the uttermost – completely, perfectly, finally and for all time and eternity – those who come to God through Him, since He is always living to make petition to God and intercede with Him and intervene for them' (*Heb 7:25, Amplified Bible*).

In John 3:16 the word 'believe' is the hand of faith stretched out in confidence to the giver. The word 'have' is the hand of faith drawn back in contentment with the gift. The trust guarantees the transaction.

Read John 3:16 out loud with empha-
sis on the words 'believe' and 'have'.
Let the richness of the text sink deep
into your spirit today.

FRIDAY 4 MARCH
Perish . . . Eternal Life

John 3:16

'For God so loved the world that he gave his one and only Son,
that whoever believes in him shall not perish but have eternal life'
(v. 16, NIV).

John 3:16 contains a word to make us tremble, the word 'perish', expressing judgment and finality. When the disciples were tossed about by the storm, they cried out to Jesus, 'Save, Lord; we are perishing' (*Matt 8:25, RSV*). The same word is used to describe what Herod planned to do with baby Jesus. 'Herod will seek the young child to destroy him' (*Matt 2:13, AV*). There is no way to pretty up this word. It means just what it says.

When the human body dies, the soul lives on, for it is immortal and programmed for eternity. We take into eternity the things that have been our soul's companions and passions in this life. If we have nurtured our soul – our inner being – with addictions and appetites, cravings and desires, lusts and loathings, these will be the awful baggage accompanying us into eternity. 'Let him who does wrong continue to do wrong; let him who is vile continue to be vile' (*Rev 22:11*).

If we have nurtured our soul – our inner being – with the mercy and forgiveness of God, trusting him for salvation, redemption and transformation, these will be the blessed companions we take with us into eternity. 'Let him who does right continue to do right; and let him who is holy continue to be holy' (*Rev 22:11*).

God's desire is that everyone should come to repentance. He does not want anyone to perish. Those who believe in God and put their trust in Jesus receive (present tense, starting now) eternal life, which is the life of God himself. 'This is the testimony,' wrote John. 'God has given us eternal life, and this life is in his Son. He who has the Son has life; he who does not have the Son of God does not have life' (*1 John 5:11,12*).

John 3:16 begins with God, the One who had no beginning, and ends with eternal life, the life that has no ending.

Read John 3:16 out loud with emphasis on the words 'perish' and 'eternal life'. Let the richness of the text sink deep into your spirit today.

SATURDAY 5 MARCH
The Power of the Text

John 3:16

'This is how much God loved the world: He gave his Son, his one and only Son. And this is why: so that no one need be destroyed; by believing in him, anyone can have a whole and lasting life' (v. 16, *The Message*).

The story is told of a youngster on a street corner in Chicago one winter's night. He asked a policeman if there was somewhere warm he could sleep for the night. The policeman pointed to a large house along the street. 'Knock on that door,' he said. 'Say "John 3:16" and see what happens.'

The boy followed the policeman's instructions. He knocked on the door and a woman opened it. 'John 3:16,' said the boy. 'Come in, son,' said the woman. She took the boy inside, sat him in a large chair by a fireplace and let him get warm. She brought him a meal, then took him upstairs to a bathroom where she ran a bath for him, and afterwards tucked him into a warm bed with clean sheets. The youngster went to sleep that night, amazed at the power of John 3:16. He thought to himself, 'I don't understand it, but it sure makes a cold boy warm and fed and bathed and rested.'

In the morning after breakfast, he asked the woman what John 3:16 meant. She opened her Bible to John's Gospel and told the boy of the God who loved him so much that he gave Jesus to die in his place so that he might have eternal life. Right there, the youngster gave his heart to Jesus. He said, 'John 3:16 – I don't understand it, but it sure makes a lost boy feel safe.'

No matter how much we examine this verse, John 3:16 will always remain a mystery. How could God love so much that he could give his only Son to die? How can everyone in the world be offered such a gift? How can that gift be received simply by an act of faith? How can it make all the difference as to where you and I spend eternity?

While we will never plumb the depths of John 3:16, for us, as for the boy on the streets of Chicago, it sure makes life worth living. May the power of this text continue to live on through your life and mine.

SUNDAY 6 MARCH
The Lord Takes Delight

<u>Psalm 149</u>

'The LORD takes delight in his people; he crowns the humble with salvation' (v. 4, NIV).

Like the other psalms that surround it, Psalm 149 begins with an invitation to praise. 'Sing to the LORD a new song . . . Let Israel rejoice . . . Let the people . . . be glad . . . Let them praise his name.' This exuberant, open-armed invitation is extended to all. No one is excluded, everyone is drawn in, every voice is needed in the great hallelujah chorus.

The psalmist lists ways of praising – with the voice, with dancing and with music. He does not spell it out, but suggests there is also a disposition of praise, a way of being that shows the centre of one's life, the focus of one's joy, to be not self but God. The psalmist gives, as a reason for praise, the Lord who 'takes delight in his people'. People praising fill God with joy.

Then suddenly, the psalm dives in another direction. References to vengeance, punishment, fetters and shackles of iron seem strangely out of place in a song of praise. These words need to be read carefully.

The whole book of Psalms makes it clear that God's saving activity in the world is carried out by people working for justice, righteousness and peace. As Jesus taught, and as he himself experienced, such things are not easily won. True power is found by surrendering power. The upward way is by the downward bend. Gain means first giving up, greatness comes by way of self-denial, glory by way of suffering.

These sober words in the second-last psalm of the Psalter are a reminder that the call to discipleship is always a call to cross-bearing. A song of praise to God will always be sung in the midst of opposition. The proclamation of God's sovereignty will always be made in the midst of circumstances that seem to deny it.

Make me a captive, Lord,
And then I shall be free;
Force me to render up my sword,
And I shall conqueror be.
I sink in life's alarms
When by myself I stand;
Imprison me within thine arms
And strong shall be my hand.
                    George Matheson, SASB 508

HABAKKUK'S STORY
Introduction

You may have difficulty locating the book of Habakkuk in your Bible. You may not find his name easy to spell, let alone pronounce. You may wonder what this unknown man from the distant past has to say to you as a believer today. You may be about to be surprised!

Like Jeremiah, Habakkuk was a prophet of God, proclaiming a bright word of hope at a dark time in history. Like Job, Habakkuk expressed anguish at the seeming injustice of God's ways. Like Amos, Habakkuk considered God to be big enough to handle gut–wrenching complaints and probing questions. Like the psalmist, Habakkuk prayed out his anguish to God, asking, 'How long?' and 'Why?'. Like Jacob, Habakkuk wrestled with God until he had an answer.

Unlike all these people, however, Habakkuk begins his book with lament and protest and ends with an overwhelming vision of God's saving presence. The book of Habakkuk contains gifts for believers today. It reminds us of the transitory reign of evil, it reassures us of the ultimate victory of God and it gives us a glimpse of what we need to do in this era in history when the Kingdom of God is already here but still coming.

Come, let us take off our shoes, like Moses before the burning bush, and step onto the holy ground of Habakkuk's story.

MONDAY 7 MARCH
The Prophet's Burden

Habakkuk 1:1

'The oracle that the prophet Habakkuk saw' (v. 1, NRSV).

Who is this man with the strange-sounding name? Where does he come from? Who nurtured him in the ways of God? Who prepared him for the task of being God's spokesman? His book gives no answers to these questions. All we are told of the man himself is contained in the first statement. Seven words give his name, his occupation and the title of his work.

Some suggest that Habakkuk's name is Babylonian, referring to a kind of garden plant. Others suggest that it is related to the Hebrew root *habhak*, meaning 'to embrace'. Luther commented that Habakkuk has the right name for his office, for his name means 'a heartener, or one who takes another to his heart and his arms, as one soothes a poor weeping child, telling him to be quiet'.

Habakkuk is described as 'the prophet' and is told to do what prophets do, namely, 'Write down the revelation and make it plain' (2:2). His task is to express clearly what God is saying. The book closes with a musical ascription (3:19b), which may suggest that Habakkuk was also a Levite, involved with worship at the temple.

Habakkuk's message is called an oracle. This word means a 'burden', something that has been lifted up and is being carried. Many of the Old Testament prophets declared a message of God's judgment that was burdensome and heavy to carry. This oracle is not Habakkuk's own opinion, but a God-given message that cannot be ignored. It is one which the prophet has received (*NIV*), or, more accurately, 'seen' (*NRSV*). There are many references in this book to watching, looking and seeing. The prophet is a see-er, one who reads and interprets God's message. Habakkuk is a man with his eyes wide open, both to the heavy burden God has given him and to what he must do with it.

To reflect on

'Cast your burden on the LORD,' says the psalmist (Ps 55:22, NRSV). That is, roll back on him what he has rolled on to you. What God-given burden do you need God's help to carry today?

TUESDAY 8 MARCH
How Long, O Lord?

Habakkuk 1:2–4

'How long, O Lord, must I call for help, but you do not listen?'
(v. 2, NIV).

Habakkuk's age-old questions are as up-to-date as this morning's paper. 'Why does an intruder get compensation for his injuries?' 'Why do three men get off scot-free from a murder they obviously committed?' 'Why do people have to move out of their homes to avoid the toxic effects of aerial spraying?' 'How long will long be, Lord, when long already feels too long?'

The agonising issues of Habakkuk's day were not global warming, rising road-crash statistics or genetically modified organisms in food. His world was the late seventh century BC when the nation of Judah was being afflicted by corruption within and oppressors without. Good King Josiah had been followed by Jehoahaz and Jehoiakim who were both ambitious, corrupt kings. Nineveh, the capital of Assyria, had fallen, but Babylon was quickly becoming the dominant world power and a threat to Judah.

Habakkuk had a vision of a dying world and it broke his heart. Everywhere he looked, he saw violence. The poor and underprivileged were being exploited by the rich and powerful. Judah's judicial system was in disarray, with quarrels and lawsuits everywhere but justice nowhere to be seen. Worst of all, the law (in Hebrew *torah*) was paralysed. God's law as the basis for personal and social behaviour was not merely being ignored, but deliberately perverted. As a result, 'the wicked hem in the righteous' (v. 4), far outnumbering God's people, surrounding them on every side. The whole fabric of society was unravelling, giving way to anarchy and lawlessness.

Habakkuk felt trapped by the violence of the wicked. God's covenant people, far from being helped and blessed, were desperate and defenceless. The prophet reminded God that he had been crying out for answers for a long time, but God seemed not to be listening.

To reflect on

Habakkuk's description of the wicked hemming in the righteous is in contrast to the psalmist who said, 'You [God] hem me in – behind and before; you have laid your hand upon me' (Ps 139:5). What hems you in, holds you firm, hedges you about today? Give thanks for God's protection and covering.

WEDNESDAY 9 MARCH
God's Fearful Answer

Habakkuk 1:5–11

'Look at the nations and watch – and be utterly amazed.
For I am going to do something in your days that you would not
believe, even if you were told' (v. 5, NIV).

Habakkuk's anguished cry of 'How long?' is answered speedily. God commands the prophet to open his eyes and look beyond Judah to see what God is doing on a much broader horizon. The message to the prophet is so amazing and dramatic that it is told, not just in words, but in a series of fast–moving, powerful images.

God's revelation to Habakkuk begins with reference to a foreign nation. The name 'Chaldean' refers to the Neo–Babylonian empire which was founded by Nabopolassar around 626 BC. When his son Nebuchadnezzar came to the throne in 605 BC, the Babylonians became a world power. Nebuchadnezzar captured and destroyed Jerusalem, thus ending the southern kingdom of Judah in 587 BC (see 2 Kgs 24:8–25:21). The Babylonians soon ruled over Assyria, Syria, Palestine and Egypt. Yet, less than fifty years after the destruction of Jerusalem, this ancient superpower fell as quickly as it had risen, conquered without resistance in 539 BC by Cyrus II, king of Persia.

The amazing, shocking message given to Habakkuk is that this great superpower is going to be the means of God's judgment on Judah. These 'ruthless and impetuous people' are described in graphic terms. Feared and dreaded, a law unto themselves, promoting their own honour, they ride horses swifter than leopards, fiercer than hungry wolves at dusk, swooping like scavenging vultures.

Habakkuk's despairing cry of 'Violence!' within Judah is about to be answered. A conquering power is coming 'bent on violence', advancing like the desert wind, laughing at anything that stands in its way. This fearful army will rush through Judah from one end to the other, gathering prisoners like sand.

These powerful, poetic images are a dramatic answer to Habakkuk's cry to God. There is no comfort here, no reassurance. It is as if God is saying, 'You think things are bad? You haven't seen anything yet!'

To reflect on
What do you do when you think your situation cannot possibly get any worse, and it does? Where do you hide when hopelessness mixes with helplessness and discouragement turns to despair? Where is a refuge to be found?

THURSDAY 10 MARCH
Horror and Hope

Habakkuk 1:12–2:1

'O LORD, are you not from everlasting? My God, my Holy One, we will not die. O LORD, you have appointed them to execute judgment; O Rock, you have ordained them to punish' (v. 12, NIV).

Habakkuk is horrified to hear what God has spoken. The thought of the Babylonians with their evil tactics being used to execute God's judgment against Judah is simply unbelievable.

He responds with a question that is, in fact, an affirmation of faith. This verse has been called 'one of the noblest in the Old Testament'. It speaks of the eternal, unchangeable, holy character of God. 'O LORD, are you not from everlasting? My God, my Holy One' (v. 12). Note the possessive pronouns here. This verse lays bare the intercessory heart of the prophet.

Habakkuk sounds like David, who declared, 'I love you, O LORD, my strength. The LORD is my rock, my fortress and my deliverer' (Ps 18:1,2). He sounds like Paul, who wrote to the Philippians, 'My God will meet all your needs according to his glorious riches in Christ Jesus' (Phil 4:19). To pray for others, we must first have a personal grasp, a first-hand knowledge, of God for ourselves.

That God will use the Babylonians to punish Judah is unbelievable to the prophet. That God is still in control, working out his purposes, is indisputable. 'O LORD, you have appointed them ... O Rock, you have ordained them.' While Habakkuk queries the process, he has no quarrel with the Person.

In a spirit of faith that knows God well enough to trust him in spite of the most persistent doubts, Habakkuk launches into his second complaint. His objection is simply that those who come to carry out God's judgment are even more wicked than those they are punishing. He compares the Babylonians to fishermen catching fish with hooks and scooping them up in dragnets. The fish are helpless and defenceless, the angler gloating as he sweeps and fills his net again and again.

In the Babylonians' dominance, however, lie the seeds of their own downfall. They worship their own power. They see themselves as unconquerable and indestructible. Will God really allow this arrogant enemy to destroy his people? Habakkuk stands, waits and watches for God's answer.

Pray today for someone who faces injustice, oppression or personal tragedy.

FRIDAY 11 MARCH
Waiting for God's Answer

Habakkuk 2:1–4

'The revelation awaits an appointed time; it speaks of the end and will not prove false. Though it linger, wait for it; it will certainly come and will not delay' (v. 3, NIV).

The prophet wants to be in the best possible position to receive God's message, so he climbs up to a high place. 'I will station myself on the ramparts,' he says. Stone watchtowers were often built on city walls so that watchmen could see enemies or messengers approaching the city, while they were still at a distance.

The psalmist cried, 'From the ends of the earth I call to you, I call as my heart grows faint; lead me to the rock that is higher than I' (*Ps 61:2*). Just as climbing a hill or the winding steps of a cathedral tower gives us a different perspective on what lies beneath, so prayer in a high place helps us to see our situation differently, as if from God's perspective.

In his high place, Habakkuk is told to do two things – write and wait. He is to inscribe the vision God gives him onto tablets so that the message is clear and intelligible to all. Then he is to wait. Even if, humanly speaking, the vision seems to be delayed in coming, God assures him it will come. It will not be one moment too late. The prophet's writing must be clear, his waiting confident. He is called to live by faith (*v. 4*), that is, resting in the faithfulness of God.

Habakkuk lived in the in-between time, often called the 'gap', between the vision being given and being fulfilled, somewhere along the line of predicament, promise and resolution. Like the prophet, Christians today also live in the gap. We live in the already–here–but–still–coming kingdom of God. Jesus has come, but we await his next, full and final coming when all things will be reconciled to God. In the meantime, like the prophet, we watch and wait and pray, 'Your kingdom come, your will be done on earth as it is in heaven' (*Matt 6:10*).

To reflect on
Do you have a watchtower, a high place of prayer where you bring your needs to God and wait for his answers? What do you pray and wait for from God today?

SATURDAY 12 MARCH
The Fall of Tyranny

Habakkuk 2:5–14

'The earth will be filled with the knowledge of the glory of the LORD, as the waters cover the sea' (v. 14, NIV).

The prophet knows the vision will come. God has assured him it will not delay unduly. Yet he must wait. The remaining verses of this chapter contain a series of five charges against the tyrannical nation of Babylon. The speaker here is neither the prophet nor God, but rather the nations who have been overrun and who now break their silence to address their oppressor.

Babylon is condemned for the exorbitant and ill-gotten wealth it has gained by taking captives from all the nations (v. 5). The tables will be turned against this arrogant superpower, reducing it to nothing more than an object of taunt and ridicule. Babylon will itself be plundered by the very people it has plundered. The victor will become the victim (vv. 6–8).

Imagining itself to be safe and untouchable, Babylon will face a punishment coming from within, from the very walls and woodwork of its homes (vv. 9–11). Conquering cities by bloodshed and rebuilding them will ultimately bring Babylon no profit. Revenue gained from the blood and sweat of others will only feed the flames of its own judg-ment. A flood of violence and bloodshed will give way to a flood of knowledge of the glory of God (see *Isa 11:9*).

These verses are not easy to read as devotional material for they speak of a particular dark time in history. But the message underlying these verses is a common theme in Scripture, namely that evil and tyranny do not have and will not have the last word. In the end, the evil that a nation or an individual inflicts upon another will come back upon itself.

While evil seems to have an upper hand, while tyranny appears to triumph, while bad things happen to good people, these victories are just for the moment. In the end, God promises, the whole earth will be filled with the knowledge of his glory. It is for this vision that believers, you and I, work and wait and pray today.

Jesus shall conquer, lift up the strain!
Evil shall perish and righteousness shall reign.
Albert Orsborn, SASB 173

SUNDAY 13 MARCH

The Great Crescendo

Psalm 150

'Let everything that has breath praise the LORD. Praise the LORD'
(v. 6, NIV).

Psalm 150 is the final doxology (literally 'word of glory') in the book of Psalms. As the psalm is sung, the volume of praise is increased with the addition of the sound of each musical instrument until it reaches a great crescendo.

Where is the Lord to be praised? In heaven, as well as in his sanctuary on earth – that is, in all the places where God's people worship him. *Why is the Lord to be praised?* Because of his acts of power, his mighty deeds in creation, history and redemption, and for his awesome majesty and greatness.

How is the Lord to be praised? With wind, stringed and percussion instruments, with sacred dance and with human voices. *By whom is the Lord to be praised?* By all human beings and by everything that lives and breathes. The whole universe is one great temple in which all the creatures of God are called to worship. Each succeeding generation will add its own cries of 'Amen!' and 'Glory!'.

This is the last magnificent *Hallelujah* in the book of Psalms. It is a foretaste of the heavenly *Hallelujah* that will sound with the final great victory of God. 'Then I heard what sounded like a great multitude, like the roar of rushing waters and like loud peals of thunder, shouting: "Hallelujah! For our Lord God Almighty reigns. Let us rejoice and be glad and give him glory!" ' (*Rev* 19:6–7).

The book of Psalms is a reflection of the journey of life that winds its way through dips and dangers, longings and laments, surprises and sorrows. When all has been said and done, the psalmist's conclusion is that to live is to praise God and to praise God is to live. In this long journey, Psalm 150 is the climactic crescendo, the final breathtaking note.

All creatures of our God and King,
Lift up your voice and with us sing
  Alleluia, alleluia!
Thou burning sun with golden beam,
Thou silver moon with softer gleam:

  O praise him, O praise him,
  Alleluia, alleluia, alleluia!
                Francis of Assisi, SASB 2

MONDAY 14 MARCH

Hush! Be Silent!

Habakkuk 2:15–20

'The LORD is in his holy temple; let all the earth be silent before him'
(v. 20, NIV).

The woes against Babylon continue. The tyrant nation is condemned for becoming rich by making others poor. Babylon has pursued glory, honour and security by using violent and unjust means. Her violence has reached even the majestic cedars of Lebanon, symbols of greatness and glory in the ancient world. Lebanon's forests have been ravaged, trees felled and the wood used to adorn Babylon's temples and palaces. Animals that once lived in the forests have also been destroyed. No form of life has been spared from this conquering nation.

Two images of shame – drunkenness and nakedness – tell the bitter end of her story. Babylon's violence against her neighbours, which stripped them of all their wealth, will be turned back on herself. 'Now it is your turn!' (v. 16). What she has done to others will be done to her. Glory will be covered with disgrace. The cup of suffering from which this nation forced others to drink will now be forced on herself. Babylon, once 'a gold cup in the LORD's hand' to punish the nations (Jer 51:7), must now take her own medicine.

This is a picture of sin falling into the trap of its own making. The reign of Babylon, the cruel and unjust tyrant, will be merely passing and transitory. No matter how overwhelming evil may seem, it will not have the final word.

Symbolic of Babylon's futility are the absurd idols she worships. Man–made 'godlets', Babylon's idols are speechless, deaf and lifeless. No matter how beautifully or ornately they have been made, they are without breath, without substance, without life–giving spirit.

The prophet puts his finger to his lips and says with a note of awe, 'But the LORD is in his holy temple.' In contrast to Babylon's dumb idols, the Lord is real, he has life and he is about to speak.

To reflect on

When the knowledge of the glory of God (v. 14) comes upon an individual, it brings with it the acknowledgment that glory sought in any other way will only lead to futility. Has it been so for you?

TUESDAY 15 MARCH

The Coming of the Warrior God

Habakkuk 3:1–7

'LORD, I have heard of your fame; I stand in awe of your deeds,
O LORD. Renew them in our day, in our time make them known'
(v. 2, NIV).

The vision promised (2:2–3) finally comes to the prophet (3:3–15) who records it in the form of a prayer. The reference to *shigionoth* (v. 1) denotes a kind of sung prayer that was used as part of the liturgy in temple worship (see *Ps 7:1*). In many ways, this last chapter of Habakkuk's book is a psalm, both in style and with its reference to the musical director and to stringed instruments (v. 19b).

Like the psalms, this chapter contains both praise and petition. 'LORD, I have heard of your fame,' he says. Habakkuk may have heard tell the greatness of God in the temple, but he has also heard it in his own heart. He sounds like Job, who declared at the end of his long story of loss and learning, 'My ears had heard of you but now my eyes have seen you' (*Job 42:5*). A passed-on report has become a personal reality.

Having heard the great deeds of God in the past, the prophet begs God to 'renew' them. 'Do it again, Lord,' he cries. 'Do it again.' He appeals to God's nature of compassion and mercy to come once again to save his suffering people. The prophet, now in the style of poet, weaves together the imagery of warfare and nature to describe how God broke into history in the Exodus story.

God's glory covered the heavens and his praise filled the earth. His splendour was like sunrise, with rays flashing from his hands. Plagues ahead of him and pestilence coming behind formed his military escort. God's very coming shook the earth, causing mountains and hills to collapse and making the nations tremble. Cushan and Midian, two southern peoples, trembled in fear and fled.

This great poetry with its dramatic effects sounds like something out of *Star Wars*. This is the picture of the Warrior God marching to war, saving his people and clearing the way to his final destination.

To reflect on

Is this image of the Warrior God one that you find helpful? What would your prayer be like to such a God today?

WEDNESDAY 16 MARCH
God of Salvation

Habakkuk 3:8–15

'You came out to deliver your people, to save your anointed one. You crushed the leader of the land of wickedness, you stripped him from head to foot' (v. 13, NIV).

As Habakkuk waits and watches, he sees with the eye of a prophet a battle of life and death unfolding. He uses imagery of thunderstorms and torrents of water to describe this tumult. His verbs are powerful, full of movement; his adjectives dramatic and vivid. This description of God striding out against evil needs larger than everyday words.

The prophet addresses God directly (v. 8). The storm has broken. The divine Warrior uses clouds and rain and thunderbolts to fight against rivers and seas. Arrows of lightning streak from the bared bow of God at his thunderous command. Streams hurled from heaven tear open the parched and crumbling earth. At the appearance of the divine Warrior, the mountains quake. The torrents increase. The great ocean roars and churns up its waves. In the heavens the sun and moon stand still as lightning flashes forth like flying arrows.

In indignation and anger, God, the royal and holy One, strides through the earth, marching as to war against the armies of evil. He comes bringing salvation and deliverance to his people. Crushing,

stripping, piercing, God's power is shown against every power that opposes his rule.

These dramatic verses can be read on several different levels. There are references to creation when God made the heavens and the earth and set order and rhythm in place. There are references here to God coming to the rescue of his people in bondage in Egypt, leading them out into freedom, parting the Red Sea before them, but drowning the chariots of Egypt in the waters.

The reference to 'your anointed one' (v. 13) reaches ahead to Jesus who came from the heart of God, entered into the sinfulness of human existence and defeated the principalities and powers that held us all in bondage. In Christ, death itself has been conquered by the One who offered himself up in death, thus setting us free (see *Rom 5:6–8*).

To reflect on
Read these verses from Habakkuk as a dramatic expression of your salvation story. This is what God in Christ has done for you!

THURSDAY 17 MARCH
The Prophet Responds

Habakkuk 3:16–19

'Though the fig-tree does not bud . . . yet I will rejoice in the LORD,
I will be joyful in God my Saviour' (vv. 17,18, NIV).

Habakkuk the prophet has listened and heard. He has watched the drama of God's salvation being played out before him. Now he responds. He is not unlike Job who, after hearing God speak, declares, 'I despise myself and repent in dust and ashes' (Job 42:6). After watching the vision God has given him, Habakkuk too is brought to a place of humility, repentance and awe. With pounding heart, quivering lips and trembling legs, he makes his response to God.

His waiting and watching now (v. 16) are quite different from the stance of waiting and watching that he took earlier (2:1). Then it was to see what God would say to his question, 'Why does evil seem to have the upper hand?' Now he stands, not with an exact answer to his question, but with a vision of God's power at work, trampling down all enemies and showing beyond any doubt that evil does not have the upper hand. Habakkuk's bold declaration of faith is both poetry and prayer.

'Even if . . .,' he says. Even if it turns out to be a bad season for figs, grapes and olives, even if the

crops out in the field come to nothing, even if the sheep get dropsy and the cattle starve to death, I will rejoice in the Lord. Even if the blessings that usually come from God fail to show up, even if suffering and loss fill our days and torment our nights, even if the whole economy collapses, I will be joyful in God my Saviour.

What makes this prophet write with such serene confidence when Judah is still in sin, when Babylon is still a looming threat on the horizon, when whatever is bad today is sure to be worse tomorrow? Like the men and women of faith listed in the book of Hebrews, all that Habakkuk has seen of God gives him courage for all he has not yet seen.

May God give you and me today a Habakkuk-like faith in the ultimate victory of God, in spite of all the appearances to the contrary.

FRIDAY 18 MARCH

Even if

Habakkuk 3:16–19

'The Sovereign LORD is my strength; he makes my feet like the feet of a deer, he enables me to go on the heights' (v. 19, NIV).

Even if there are no phone messages waiting when I get in
Even if there are no emails lined up for my attention
Even if there are no notes of encouragement in today's mail
Even if no one makes an appointment to come and see me
Even if no one lines up for my autograph
Even if no one from the media requests an interview
　　or asks me to pose for a photograph
Even if no one thanks me for the work I have done today

Even if no outer voice tells me how
　great
　clever
　popular
　important
　successful
　appreciated
　or in demand I am

Even if no one seems to value what I value
and I interpret it to mean that no one values me

Lord God, even if none of these things happen
I still want to live this day to the full
bringing to my task all the excellence I can muster
flinging it out like seeds thrown from a high place
flying forth and landing where you design

Help me to choose carefully the voices I listen to
to be a space in which you can act
to let your word in my life
speak my value
and tell me exactly who I am.

SATURDAY 19 MARCH
The Final Word

Habakkuk 1:2–4; 3:19

'The Sovereign LORD is my strength; he makes my feet like the feet of a deer, he enables me to go on the heights' (v. 19, NIV).

Habakkuk's story begins with anguish. 'How long, O LORD, must I call for help, but you do not listen?' It ends with confidence. 'The Sovereign LORD is my strength; he makes my feet like the feet of a deer, he enables me to go on the heights.' Between anguish and confidence there is a long journey of listening, waiting and watching.

Habakkuk, prophet to Judah from 612 to 588 BC, lived at a time of fear, oppression, persecution, lawlessness and immorality. He could not understand why God seemed to do nothing about the wickedness in society. Was God indifferent? Why did he allow injustice to triumph? Overwhelmed with sorrow, Habakkuk poured out his questions to God.

Far from being silent, God answered. He gave the prophet a vision that helped him to understand the problem of injustice in the world and, at the same time, to maintain confidence in the just and righteous rule of God. From a place of prayer, waiting and watching, Habakkuk saw that evil has only a temporary reign. In a dramatic vision of God, the divine Warrior striding out against evil and wrongdoing, Habakkuk saw the ultimate victory of God over every opposing force.

The prophet's anguished question, 'How long?' is still a struggle for believers today. Like the prophet, we live in the midst of darkness and injustice. For all that we understand of God and God's ways, there is much we do not yet understand. With one hand we hold firmly the things we can be sure of, and with the other hand open we hold lightly the mystery of all that is still puzzling. One day the questions will all be answered. One day the mystery will clear, like sun breaking through on a foggy morning.

In the meantime, our call, like the prophet's, is to watch and wait and pray, to live with an openness of heart, with all our senses on alert. God's victory is certain. God will have the final word.

Hear then our answer: Lord, lead us on
Fighting nor resting until thy war is won.

Will Brand, SASB 864

SUNDAY 20 MARCH
Palm Sunday – He Comes

John 12:12–19

'Blessed is he who comes in the name of the Lord!' (v. 13, NIV).

He came
one ink–black night lit by a lone star
Mary's gentle lamb
ruddy flesh wrapped in rags
Joseph kneeling in wonder at this dream child
a stable echoing
his first whimpering cries

He comes this day
pale and weary on a donkey
the King of Israel
wrapped in cloaks and palm branches
to the cries of a fickle crowd
their hosanna shouts
soon echoing crucify
over Jerusalem's olive groves

He will come one day of days
not as lamb but as Lion
no select audience of two or three
but every eye drawn to welcome him
every knee bowed in adoration
He will come
wrapped in splendour
crowned with glory
King of Kings and Lord of Lords!

Add your voice to the song of praise that welcomes Jesus on this Palm Sunday.

THE EASTER JOURNEY

Introduction

Commissioner Lalkiamlova is the guest contributor for this series of Easter readings. The Commissioner is the International Secretary for South Asia. His previous appointment was as Territorial Commander for the India Central Territory, based in Chennai.

Commissioner Lalkiamlova writes:

There is nothing more wonderful for a Christian believer than the victory gained through the suffering, death and resurrection of Jesus. Death is a terrifying prospect for many people. On the other hand, life is the utmost blessing for all human beings. Let us take an example from the Old Testament. Jacob had already lived for 130 years, but he spoke as though he wanted to live still longer. He said to Pharaoh, 'The years of my pilgrimage are a hundred and thirty. My years have been few and difficult, and they do not equal the years of the pilgrimage of my fathers' (*Gen 47:9*). Jacob obviously had no understanding of life after death.

It was to overcome the fear of death and to give assurance of life after death that Jesus suffered, died and rose again. By his death on the cross he pronounced victory over death, eternal life rather than endless existence. His death and resurrection assure us that anyone who believes in him, though dead physically, will still live. The readings for this Easter season are to help Christians in their understanding about the completed work of Jesus on the cross. The eternal plan of God the Father in Jesus and the deep submission of Jesus to his Father to fulfil his mission are the truths we will concentrate on.

MONDAY 21 MARCH

Do This in Remembrance of Me

Luke 22:14–20

'And he took bread, gave thanks and broke it, and gave it to them, saying, "This is my body given for you; do this in remembrance of me" ' (v. 19, NIV).

Although he was a great teacher, Jesus did not establish any institution to teach his disciples. A city, a village, the seaside or the countryside became his places of teaching. He used nature – trees, mountains, rivers, fields, animals, birds – and whatever he could see as illustrations for the lessons he taught. He took the disciples to different places according to the lessons he wanted to teach them.

Knowing that the end of his earthly life was near, he decided to teach his final lesson, one that would demand their very lives, in a private place. As they reclined at the table at this last supper together, he said to his disciples, 'I have eagerly desired to eat this Passover with you before I suffer. For I tell you, I will not eat it again until it finds fulfilment in the kingdom of God.'

Then he took the cup and gave thanks and said, 'Take this and divide it among you. For I tell you I will not drink again of the fruit of the vine until the kingdom of God comes.' Then he took bread, gave thanks and broke it, and gave it to them, saying, 'This is my body given for you; do this in remembrance of me.'

What Jesus and his disciples drank at that supper was 'the cup of thanksgiving' for the blessing and salvation of God made available by Christ's sacrifice on the cross. The living bread that came from heaven was broken on the cross. The master died for his lambs, whereas the Old Testament required a lamb to die for its master. The new covenant could only become valid by the death of Christ.

This new covenant that Jesus made by his blood is to be followed by his disciples, too. What he offered to the world, the wine and the blood, are symbols of his life given freely, fully for all humankind. My life, too, as Albert Orsborn wrote, must be Christ's broken bread, my love his outpoured wine (*SASB 512*). May it be the same for you, too.

TUESDAY 22 MARCH

The Spirit is Willing but the Body is Weak

Mark 14:32–42

'Watch and pray so that you will not fall into temptation.
The spirit is willing, but the body is weak' (v. 38, NIV).

After supper Jesus took his disciples to the Garden of Gethsemane. The heart of Jesus was heavy, knowing that he would soon be delivered into the cruel hands of the religious leaders and then to the Roman soldiers. He knew he would be hung on a cross. His disciples did not share his agony, nor were they able to give Jesus the comfort he needed at that moment.

Moving away from the disciples, Jesus prayed to his Father that the cup of suffering be taken from him. Even in such a desperate situation he did not put pressure on his Father, but humbly submitted himself to God's will. Returning to his disciples, he found them sleeping and said to Peter, 'Simon, are you asleep? Could you not keep watch for one hour? Watch and pray so that you will not fall into temptation. The spirit is willing but the body is weak' (vv. 37,38).

Three times he moved away and each time he returned to find them sleeping. The Bible says it was because their eyes were heavy and they did not know what to say to him. Jesus' action is an example of what believers ought to do in times of great distress and grief – turn to God in prayer.

The inability of the body (the flesh) to understand the things of the spirit is clearly shown here. Jesus told them that his soul was overwhelmed with sorrow to the point of death. But the disciples could not see any reason why he should be so sorrowful. After all, they did not yet have the understanding that the infilling of the Holy Spirit would bring to them.

Sometimes Christians today are like the disciples of that time. There are many things that no eye has seen, no ear has heard, no mind has conceived, but which God has revealed to us by his Spirit. The Spirit searches all things, even the deep things of God. As we live in the Spirit, we will be able to see and understand spiritual things much more clearly (see 1 Cor 2:9,10).

WEDNESDAY 23 MARCH
Your Dead Will Live

Isaiah 26:18–21

'But your dead will live; their bodies will rise. You who dwell
in the dust, wake up and shout for joy. Your dew is like the dew of the
morning; the earth will give birth to her dead' (v. 19, NIV).

The law of Moses and the beliefs of Judaism proclaimed the desperate condition of the dead. They considered that life in this world is an utmost blessing from God. The following psalms clearly spell out the belief that what happened after death was something dark and silent: 'It is not the dead who praise the LORD, those who go down to silence' (Ps 115:17). 'Do you show your wonders to the dead? Do those who are dead rise up and praise you?' (Ps 88:10). 'No-one remembers you when he is dead. Who praises you from his grave?' (Ps 6:5).

The dead are called 'shades' (*rephaim*), not 'souls', in the Old Testament. Their abode is called *Sheol*, and in many respects it is like the Greek Hades. The concept of *Sheol* seems to have grown out of the idea of the family burial plot, probably under the influence of Babylonian ideas (see *Gen 23:19; 25:9; 49:29,30*). It is 'the house of meeting for all living', 'the land of darkness, and of the shadow of death', where the distinctions of earth, even its moral distinctions, cease to operate. 'There the wicked cease from turmoil, and there the weary are at rest. Captives also enjoy their ease; they no longer hear the slave driver's shout' (*Job 3:17,18*).

Although the Pharisees believed in life after death, the disciples of Jesus were probably not sure exactly what Jesus was saying when he spoke to them about his resurrection from the dead. In spite of his repeated teachings about his own resurrection, they still seemed to be caught by surprise when it actually happened. The resurrection of Jesus opens up a new theology about life after death. It gives a new hope to all those who believe in him. His resurrection is the guarantee that all those who die in Jesus will be resurrected like him and will be with him forever.

May this assurance from the very life of Jesus bring confidence and encouragement to your faith today. Remember, we serve a risen Saviour who is with us in the world today (*SASB 334*).

THURSDAY 24 MARCH
He Was Numbered among the Transgressors

Luke 22:31–38

'It is written: "And he was numbered with the transgressors";
and I tell you that this must be fulfilled in me' (v. 37, NIV).

From about the age of twelve Jesus was aware of his own divinity. He declared this at the temple in Jerusalem to his mother. Although he was the Son of God, he preferred to be with sinners, those whom the religious leaders detested. Jesus knew that sinners would gladly hear the gospel of repentance and forgiveness, whereas the religious leaders, although sinners themselves, would never admit to that. Repentance was the last thing on their minds.

Wherever Jesus went he mingled with sinners. They pressed in to hear what he had to say. They surrounded him closely and listened carefully to his teachings. At Jericho he saw Zacchaeus in a sycamore tree and called to him personally, saying that he wanted to go home with him and have fellowship with him. Observing how the tax collectors and the sinners drew near to Jesus to hear him, the Pharisees and the scribes complained (*Luke 15:1–2*).

One day, one of the Pharisees, called Simon, invited Jesus to eat with him. As Jesus sat down to the meal, an uninvited guest appeared. She was a woman of the city, known to be a sinner. She brought an alabaster flask of fragrant oil and stood at his feet, weeping. She washed his feet with her tears then wiped them with her hair. Then she anointed them with the fragrant oil (*Luke 7:36–38*).

Jesus commended her action. She had done for him what Simon, as host, had neglected to do. The woman knew that she was a sinner in need of forgiveness. Simon was self-righteous in his secure position as a Pharisee. He judged the woman because of her sinful ways, but Jesus forgave her because of her repentance.

It seems appropriate that Jesus died between two criminals. We too live in this world alongside sinners and transgressors, but are we living for them? In God's sight the greatest in his kingdom are those with the greatest love. Jesus commended those who would lay down their lives for their friends (*John 15:13*). That is exactly what he did. That is what he calls us to do also.

FRIDAY 25 MARCH
With Me in Paradise

Luke 23:32–43

'Jesus answered him, "I tell you the truth, today you will be with me in paradise" ' (v. 43, NIV).

Jesus was crucified on the cross in the morning (possibly around 11 a.m.). Satan and his forces were still not satisfied with the crucifixion, but mocked him in highly ironic language. There were four groups of mocking people: the rulers, the soldiers, the people passing by and one of the criminals crucified at the same time. They all used the same word, 'save', to insult Jesus. This was exactly what Jesus was doing on the cross for the whole world. But the world did not understand the language of redemption.

'Save' does not mean to escape from physical suffering. Rather, it means being saved from the wrath of God, a price that can never be paid by any human being. How painful it must have been for Jesus to hear such an insult while he was suffering such agony. The mockers spoke truth without realising what they said. Indeed, even as Jesus hung there on the cross he was carrying out God's saving, salvaging plan.

To add insult to injury, even as Jesus hung there dying, the soldiers who crucified him divided his clothes by casting lots between them. That would have been a terrible scene for Jesus. Was he aware of what they were doing? Did he recall the Scripture that foretold this very action? It is worth noting that Jesus refused to drink the wine, mixed with gall, offered to him to relieve his pain (*Matt 27:34*). It may have been that Jesus preferred to suffer pain and die forsaken, so that we might never be forsaken.

In repentance, the second criminal asked Jesus to remember him. Even in the midst of his agony, Jesus spoke a word of salvation to him. 'I tell you the truth, today you will be with me in paradise.'

'Today' speaks of the immediacy of salvation. The term 'paradise' indicates heaven or the presence of God. Jesus' words give us the clear reassurance that, after death, the saved will go immediately into Jesus' presence in heaven. This same voice of Jesus should ring in our ears, too, for repentance and redemption.

SATURDAY 26 MARCH
Prepare Me for Burial

Matthew 26:6–13

'When she poured this perfume on my body, she did it to prepare me for burial' (v. 12, NIV).

The earthly life and ministry of Jesus were part of the eternal purposes of God. Jesus himself declared that all the prophecies about him would be fulfilled. His birth, the family's flight to Egypt and their return to Israel, his death and resurrection were all in fulfilment of prophecies spoken down through the centuries.

Mary and her friends went to the tomb early in the morning. They had forgotten what Jesus had taught about his resurrection on the third day. They went to anoint his body with perfume and spices according to the Jewish custom. They had prepared these on the evening of Friday, just before the Sabbath started (see *Luke 23:56*).

The Bible records Nicodemus bringing a mixture of myrrh and aloes and wrapping the body of Jesus with spices. Mary and her friends obviously knew about this, but felt there was more to be done. So they went home, prepared their last offerings and then rested. On the first day of the week they went to the tomb early in the morning to anoint the body. They found the tomb opened and the body of Jesus not in the place where he had been laid.

We know that the body of Jesus had already been anointed by a woman with expensive perfume a few days earlier at the house of Simon the leper. As this woman poured her perfume over him, Jesus had said, 'When she poured this perfume on my body, she did it to prepare me for burial.' This woman is thought to be Mary, one of the women at the tomb on the resurrection morning. It was as if God knew there would not be enough time to follow the Jewish custom, and so the anointing took place several days before Jesus actually died.

Whatever we do for Jesus, no matter how small or simple, no matter how unnoticed by others, our closeness with Christ and our love for him are the most important and valuable aspects of that relationship. Every act of love we do is noted in the book of heaven.

SUNDAY 27 MARCH

Roll the Stone Away

John 20:1–9

'Mary Magdalene went to the tomb and saw that the stone
had been removed from the entrance' (v. 1, NIV).

This Easter mystery captures me again
The stone is rolled away
an empty tomb bids me bend
and look into the darkness

When tragedy strikes
when men use weapons instead of words
when children suffer at the hands of family
    roll the stone away
    shine the light of resurrection
    unlock the Jesus within
    let Easter come again

When fear grips my heart
when someone's cutting remark leaves me bleeding
when everything within me shouts 'No, I can't'
    roll the stone away
    shine the light of resurrection
    unlock the Jesus within
    let Easter come again

When sorrow deadens and guilt cripples
when anxiety burdens and despair overwhelms
when darkness snuffs out every flickering flame
    roll the stone away
    shine the light of resurrection
    unlock the Jesus within
    let Easter come again

    Here's to rolling stones away
    here's to wildness and wonder
    freedom and forgiveness
    hope and healing
    here's to resurrection
    let Easter come again!

MONDAY 28 MARCH

Why Look for the Living among the Dead?

Luke 24:1–8

'In their fright the women bowed down with their faces to the ground, but the men said to them, "Why do you look for the living among the dead?" ' (v. 5, NIV).

Early on that morning the women went to the tomb to anoint the body of Jesus. They wondered about the heavy stone at the entrance but when they arrived they found it had been rolled away. Looking inside, they could not see the body of Jesus. Then two men, whose clothes gleamed like lightning, suddenly stood beside the women and said, 'Why do you look for the living among the dead? He is not here; he has risen!'

Going to visit the tomb of a relative is a popular practice throughout the world. Many people go to visit the grave of their relatives and weep over it. People want to make the tomb as beautiful as possible. They may decorate the tomb by planting flowers around it or putting flowers and greenery in a vase.

On All Saints Day many Catholics and even Protestant Christians visit the graves of their dear ones and offer prayers to God for their lives on earth. This practice could be influenced by Roman Catholic teaching about purgatory. Some people believe purgatory to be a place where the souls of the dead wait until all their sins are forgiven. Those who hold this belief pray for the release of the souls of their relatives. Some do it to show how much they love the person they are remembering. Others do it because they want to do the best thing they can for those who have died. Whatever the reason for going to a tomb, or praying for the souls of the dead, the important thing to understand is that living souls are not to be found among the dead.

The words spoken by these two men brought comfort to the women and helped them to recollect all that Jesus had spoken to them while he was with them in his human form. Their words gave the women the assurance that Jesus was alive. May this truth be of great comfort to all believers today. Those who die in Jesus are not to be found among the dead, for their souls are with God.

TUESDAY 29 MARCH

He Has Risen

Matthew 28:1–10

'He is not here; he has risen, just as he said. Come and see the place where he lay' (v. 6, NIV).

It is hard to imagine Mary and the other women sleeping during the night before resurrection morning. They would hardly have needed a wake-up call or an alarm clock on the dawn of Sunday. When they went near to the tomb, wondering about the heavy stone, to their surprise the angel of the Lord appeared to them. He said, 'He is not here; he has risen, just as he said.' Then he showed them the place where Jesus had been laid. This message gave mixed feelings of fear and joy to Mary and her friends, and later to the disciples also.

The resurrected Jesus did not leave his disciples in a perplexed state, wondering about what had happened to him. What a wonderful and marvellous morning it must have been as the Master appeared and spoke with them. No other day would have been more delightful and exciting for them than that Easter morning. It was a morning that gave new hope to those whose hearts were filled with sadness and sorrow over his death. It was a morning that cheered those who had hung their heads in shame. It was a morning for the disciples to understand at last what Jesus had meant when he had talked to them about his own resurrection.

It was a morning that brought together again the disciples who had been scattered by shame and fear over the death of their Master. Their new greeting, 'He has risen', must have sounded wonderful. I can visualise the posture of the disciples in whom fear, joy, doubt, awe and even tears were mingled together when the resurrected Christ appeared before them. It must have been an amazing re-union after the bleak and perplexing period of time they had just been through.

Through his resurrection, Christ won victory over the darkness of death and defeated the power of Satan, the last enemy. Christ's resurrection makes available to every believer the presence of Christ and his power over sin. Christ's resurrection happened two thousand years ago, but the effect of it is still being felt today. Hallelujah!

WEDNESDAY 30 MARCH

He is Alive

Luke 24:13–27

'They came and told us that they had seen a vision of angels,
who said he was alive' (v. 23, NIV).

'Strike the shepherd, and the sheep will be scattered,' said the prophet Zechariah (*Zech* 13:7). This is what happened when Jesus was crucified and died. His disciples were hiding behind locked doors because they were afraid of the Jews. Cleopas and his friend were as disappointed and desperate as all the others. They were on their way home from Jerusalem, heading towards the village of Emmaus. As they walked, they talked together of how their hopes in Jesus had been dashed to pieces.

Unexpectedly, the resurrected Jesus appeared and walked with them. Failing to recognise him, the two friends told Jesus what had happened. They said in despair, 'We had hoped that he was the one who was going to redeem Israel … In addition, some of our women amazed us. They went to the tomb early this morning but didn't find his body. They came and told us that they had seen a vision of angels, who said he was alive. Then some of our companions went to the tomb and found it just as the women had said, but him they did not see.'

What sad friends they were! The most happy and joyous announcement, 'He is alive', had made them depressed. They did not understand what the absence of the body of Christ from the tomb meant. They were still helpless and confounded. It was all because of the wrong understanding and expectation they had about Jesus Christ. Not only these two friends, but the other disciples were all the same. The first thing they asked Jesus after his resurrection was, 'Lord, are you at this time going to restore the kingdom to Israel?' (*Acts* 1:6). Because of their wrong expectation the disciples were blind to the truth of what had happened, and so failed to understand what the resurrection of Jesus actually meant.

Are we any different? What expectations do we hold as we come to Jesus? Do we come to him on our terms, expecting that he will do things our way, or do we come to him on his terms, seeking only Jesus himself?

THURSDAY 31 MARCH

Stay with Us

Luke 24:28–35

'But they urged him strongly, "Stay with us, for it is nearly evening; the day is almost over." So he went in to stay with them' (v. 29, NIV).

The story is told of a certain beggar who had a bag tightly knotted at the end of his stick. Every day he sat by the roadside and earned his livelihood begging from passers-by. People asked him what was in the bag but he told them he did not know. One day some people forced him to undo his bag. He was amazed to find inside a large piece of gold. It was worth enough to feed his family and to live on for many years. At times we fail to recognise the treasure that is within our reach. At times we fail to see what is right there in our hands.

The two sorrowful friends on their way to Emmaus were rebuked by their unexpected travelling companion when he said to them, 'How foolish you are, and how slow of heart to believe all that the prophets have spoken! Did not the Christ have to suffer these things and then enter his glory?' Beginning with the teachings of Moses and the prophets, the stranger explained to them what was said in the Scriptures concerning himself.

As the three of them approached the village of Emmaus, the stranger acted as if he were going to keep going, but they urged him to stop. 'Stay with us,' they said, 'for it is nearly evening; the day is almost over.' Jesus agreed and went into their house with them. As they sat down together at the table for a meal, he took the bread, gave thanks, broke it and began to give it to them. As he did so, their eyes were opened and they recognised him. In that moment, he disappeared from their sight. Though these two friends did not at first recognise Jesus, they were comforted by his words.

After Jesus' resurrection, over the next forty days, he appeared and talked to many others, just as he did with those travellers to Emmaus. May we, like them, continue to hold firmly to his word, so that when he appears we may be confident and unashamed at his coming.

FRIDAY 1 APRIL

A Ghost Does Not Have Flesh and Bones

Luke 24:36–49

'Look at my hands and my feet. It is I myself! Touch me and see;
a ghost does not have flesh and bones, as you see I have' (v. 39, NIV).

We can hardly imagine how busy the risen Lord must have been after his resurrection. One of his first tasks was to bring his scattered flock of disciples back together again. He met the women who went to the tomb. He walked to Emmaus and revealed himself to the two disciples, who then hurried back to Jerusalem. He went to the upper room where the other disciples were gathered together.

Not only the women, but also the men disciples were frightened and confused as to what had happened. Jesus wanted to make himself known to them clearly, so he dealt patiently with their slowness and their questions. Perhaps it was not that they were hard of heart, but that the news of his resurrection was simply unbelievable.

He showed them that he had a physical body, just as before. He urged them to touch and feel his hands so that they could see he was not just a ghost. The apostle John, writing many years later, spoke his own testimony and that of the other disciples, when he declared that they themselves had heard him with their own ears, seen him with their own eyes and touched him with their own hands (1 John 1:1).

It is important that what we proclaim to the world is what we ourselves know to be true. Our testimony, to be real, must be of what we ourselves have experienced of the risen Jesus. Only then will our witness have power. Only then will it sound authentic and true.

It is also important that our love towards others is not merely shown in words but also in actions that can be seen and touched. Such love towards others may sometimes be doubted or rejected by the people we try to love. It will be necessary to deal with such people as patiently as Jesus did with his doubting disciples. May the resurrected Jesus be a reality in whom the wandering soul and sceptical heart may find rest and comfort.

I know that my redeemer lives,
What joy the blest assurance gives!
Samuel Medley, SASB 144

SATURDAY 2 APRIL

Peace Be with You

John 20:19–23

'Peace be with you! As the Father has sent me, I am sending you'
(v. 21, NIV).

As Jesus approached Jerusalem, he wept over it. He said, 'If you, even you, had only known on this day what would bring you peace – but now it is hidden from your eyes' (*Luke 19:41,42*). He was the king of peace who would bring peace to his people, but his own people did not understand the kind of peace he brought. They thought of peace as the absence of war. But the peace Jesus brings is the wholeness of relationship and welfare that God gives to all those who submit to him.

Because the Jewish people re-fused to accept God's way of peace, they lost their grip on what fragile peace they had. The whole volatile situation blew up in their faces, leaving them with no city, no temple and eventually no nation. So Jesus wept.

After his resurrection, he went to a small group of followers whom he himself had trained to carry on his unfinished work. He offered them the peace that he brought for the world. That was exactly what they needed as they were all in hiding behind locked doors. They were confused by the death of their Master, afraid of the religious leaders and all the Jews. But when Jesus showed them his hands and side, the disciples were overjoyed to recognise him and to receive the blessing of his peace.

Just as Jesus himself had been sent into the world, he now sent them out into the world, carrying his peace with them. With that he breathed on them and said, 'Receive the Holy Spirit. If you forgive anyone his sins, they are forgiven; if you do not forgive them, they are not forgiven.' The same peace and authority to forgive sins is given to us. 'Receive the Holy Spirit' is an imperative, a command. The Holy Spirit is given to regenerate people and to make them new creatures. We must receive the Holy Spirit and the peace that he brings before we can offer anything of value to the world. May you know the joy of receiving Jesus' peace into your life today.

SUNDAY 3 APRIL

A Song of Times

Ecclesiastes 3:1–11

'There is a time for everything, and a season for every activity under heaven' (v. 1, NIV).

This passage from Ecclesiastes is read at infant dedications, weddings and funerals. It pictures human life as a tapestry, woven not with threads, but with 'times'. There is indeed a time for everything, and a season for every activity under heaven.

Twenty-eight items in fourteen pairs of opposites are listed. These multiples of seven are significant, for seven is the number of completion in Scripture. The first pair, 'a time to be born and a time to die', represent the bookends of life. Between these two come all the other aspects of human activity – planting and uprooting, creating and destroying, gathering and scattering. These activities are carried out to the accompaniment of the full range of human emotions – weeping and laughing, mourning and dancing.

The last verse of the poem features the human experiences of love and hate, war and peace, but the order of the final pair is reversed so that peace is put at the end, like a punchline. In this way, birth (v. 2) and peace (v. 8) bracket the whole list. Death, killing, scattering, tearing down and war, while all inevitable parts of the human experience, have neither the first nor the final word.

There is strong movement in these verses – inwards and outwards, upwards and downwards. Like the ebb and flow of the tide or the coming and going of the seasons, our lives have a rhythm and an order to them. Life is more than this present moment, bigger than yesterday's argument or tomorrow's worries.

The God who created us knew all the days we would live even before our lives began (Ps 139:16). He made us like trees planted along a river bank, with work to do in every season (Ps 1:3). We are set in a particular time and place and context today, but our hearts are programmed for eternity (Eccl 3:11).

In his time, in his time,
He makes all things beautiful in his time.
Lord, please show me every day
As you're teaching me your way
That you do just what you say
In your time.

Diane Ball, 'In His Time'⁵

THE HEARTLAND OF DISCIPLESHIP –
LUKE 13–16
Introduction

These chapters of Luke's Gospel are full of colour and rich detail. Jesus takes every opportunity, at a meal table or on the road, to teach, to heal, to warn. He speaks of judgment and mercy, repentance and faith. He uses stories and parables of seeds and yeast, doors and banquets, sheep and coins to paint graphic word pictures of the kingdom of God. These chapters are the heartland of discipleship – what it means, what it costs, where it will lead.

Where it is leading Jesus is towards Jerusalem. He knows he is on his way to suffering and death, so his words are not just abstract, theological theories. There is no time for such things. He lives out what he teaches. He warns his followers of opposition they will encounter, even as he faces it himself. He issues a call to integrity and faithfulness, and models these very qualities in his dealings with women and poor people. Most unforgettably, he tells the story of a father who watches, waits, then runs to embrace the son who had turned away in rebellion, but now returns home.

Read these chapters with reverence. Imagine yourself with Jesus on the road to Jerusalem. Listen to his teaching. Hear how he responds to criticism. Receive his healing touch. Let yourself be found by the waiting, welcoming Father.

MONDAY 4 APRIL
A Call to Repent

Luke 13:1–5

'I tell you, no! But unless you repent, you too will all perish'
(v. 5, NIV).

Jesus, ever the Teacher, uses everything that happens to speak truth to his audience. An incident is reported to him, telling of a group of Galileans whom Pilate slaughtered while they were in the temple offering sacrifices. Such a shocking event was consistent with Pilate's reputation. The historian Josephus reported that Pilate's troops killed a group of Samaritans climbing Mount Gerizim. He seized temple treasury funds in order to build an aqueduct. He introduced Roman effigies into Jerusalem.

The question around the incident is, 'Did those Galileans suffer in that gruesome way because they were worse-than-normal sinners?' Another story is told of eighteen people who died when a tower in the area of Siloam fell on them. The question again is, 'Is calamity God's punishment for sin?'

Job's friends certainly thought so. 'Who, being innocent, has ever perished? Where were the upright ever destroyed?' asked Eliphaz (Job 4:7). Jesus' disciples thought the same thing. 'Who sinned?' they asked when they saw a man who had been born blind. 'This man or his parents?' (John 9:2).

The logic behind such questions is that if God is responsible for everything that happens, and God is a just God, then calamities must be the result of human sinfulness. But such logic takes no account of human freedom and choice. Jesus offers no theological explanation for the two specific incidents, but points his hearers to a larger truth. 'I tell you, unless you repent, you too will all perish.' Life is uncertain, death comes when it does, judgment is inevitable.

God, it seems, has no grades of sin. There are no 'betters and worsers' when it comes to sin. We might think that adultery and murder are the biggies and white lies and gossip the tiddlers, but God sees sin simply as sin which needs to be repented of by every individual.

To reflect on
If only we could put all the bad people in one place and let God deal with them, surely that would solve the problem of evil in the world. The trouble is that evil goes right through every human heart.

TUESDAY 5 APRIL
An Unproductive Tree

Luke 13:6–9

'A man had a fig-tree, planted in his vineyard, and he went to look for fruit on it, but did not find any' (v. 6, NIV).

Jesus tells the parable of a man who planted a tree in his vineyard. For three years he looked for fruit – time enough for a tree to produce – but he found none. Three years of patience, three years of ample opportunity. Land was precious, so an unfruitful tree could not be left just to take up space that would more usefully nourish a fruitful tree. The man ordered the gardener to cut the tree down. The gardener, however, interceded on behalf of the tree, offering to dig it around and fertilise it. Then, if the tree did not bear fruit in one more year, he would cut it down. One year of mercy added to three years of patience. –

Jesus tells the story and invites the people to identify with the fig tree that is given one last chance. In the Old Testament, a fig tree or a vineyard commonly represented the nation of Israel. But it also had a personal application. The point of Jesus' parable is that, for both the nation as a whole and for people individually, the time is short.

A fruitful tree is a symbol of godly living. 'Blessed is the man who trusts in the LORD ... He will be like a tree planted by the water that sends out its roots by the stream ... and never fails to bear fruit' (Jer 17:7,8). An unfruitful tree is like a person who does not put down deep roots into the rich soil of God's word and who does not bear fruit in season.

This is a parable about accountability and the expectation of fruitfulness. What is the Lord's expectation of you today? Not to be other than who you are. Not to do other than what he has given you to do. But to be fully, wholly yourself, drawing deeply from his rich resources.

'Think of yourself as a little seed planted in rich soil. All you have to do is to stay there and trust that the soil contains everything you need to grow.'
Henri Nouwen,
The Inner Voice of Love[6]

WEDNESDAY 6 APRIL

Imagine!

Luke 13:10–13

'When Jesus saw her, he called her forward and said to her, "Woman, you are set free from your infirmity" ' (v. 12, NIV).

Imagine being bent over for eighteen years. Imagine all those years of crookedness and pain. Imagine the bones of your spine being so rigidly fused together that you cannot walk properly and can only shuffle along. Imagine never seeing trees dancing in the breeze, birds dipping and soaring, clouds playing tag in the sky. Imagine the landscape of every day being dust and worms, stones and cracked earth.

Imagine people telling you it is because of your sin that you are bent over like this. Imagine being an object of curiosity, the recipient of people's cold sympathy, always being overlooked, ignored, left out. Imagine being known, not for your character, but for your crookedness. Imagine hearing, 'Oh, here she comes again,' when you make your way to market each day.

Imagine studying your grandchildren's feet but never their faces. Imagine hearing laughter but never seeing the joke; other people's conversation going literally over your head; the lonely world you would retreat to. Imagine being a dark question mark on a grey page.

Imagine one day hearing a voice calling and someone saying to you, 'Woman, you're free!' (v. 12, The Message). Imagine feeling strong hands on your shoulder and back as someone speaks blessing over you then gently helps you to straighten. Imagine uncurling the question mark of your body and standing up like an exclamation mark! Imagine feeling normal again, alive and whole for the first time in eighteen years!

Imagine this woman looking you in the eye today and telling you her story. Imagine her asking you what bends you over, what lays such a heavy burden on your back that you can see only footprints and failure, dust and discouragement, sticks and stones. Imagine her taking you by the hand and leading you over to where Jesus is standing. 'Jesus, I want you to meet my friend,' she says, introducing you. You look up into eyes that are gentle and strong. You feel the warmth of his hand on your shoulder. You see him smile. You hear him say to you, 'You're free!'

Imagine!

THURSDAY 7 APRIL
A Sabbath Healing

Luke 13:14–17

'Should not this woman, a daughter of Abraham, whom
Satan has kept bound for eighteen long years, be set free on the
Sabbath day from what bound her?' (v. 16, NIV).

The instant healing of the woman who has been bent over for eighteen years would be cause for immediate rejoicing, except for one fact – it is the Sabbath.

While Jesus is delighted with her healing and the woman herself stands straight and praises God, the synagogue ruler has an altogether different reaction. He is indignant ('furious', *The Message*). There are six days for work, he says. So come and be healed on one of those days but not on the Sabbath. He sees not the victim of crookedness, nor the victory of healing, but the violation of a rule. In the moment of her healing, the woman suddenly becomes an issue, a point of contention, Exhibit A in a legal battle.

The synagogue ruler argues that the healing could have waited. Jesus has violated laws of working on the Sabbath (see *Exod 20:9–10*). In the *Mishnah*, a book of Jewish tradition, there is a list of thirty-nine activities prohibited for the Sabbath. A person could travel only so far, although it was permitted to lead cattle to water.

Jesus responds sternly, addressing the synagogue ruler and those who side with him as 'hypocrites'. They untie an animal that has been bound and lead it to water on the Sabbath. How much more should this woman who has been crippled by Satan for eighteen years be unbound and given her freedom? What more appropriate day could there be for restoring dignity to a daughter of Abraham, a woman standing in the line of promise? Surely the Sabbath is the best of all days to defeat Satan's power, to release people from his bondage and to celebrate the goodness and healing grace of God?

The reaction to Jesus' words to the ruler is as immediate as the woman's healing. The crowd is delighted. A ministry of compassion has been seen to take priority over rules and rigidity. Jesus' opponents are humiliated. They are now the ones standing in the place of shame, their heads bowed.

To reflect on
How is this story of the stooped woman the story of many women?

FRIDAY 8 APRIL

So Grows the Kingdom

Luke 13:18–21

'What is the kingdom of God like? . . . It is like a mustard seed . . .
It is like yeast . . . ' (vv. 18,19,21, NIV).

The Old Testament prophets described the kingdom as a great cedar. 'On the mountain heights of Israel I will plant it; it will produce branches and bear fruit and become a splendid cedar. Birds of every kind will nest in it; they will find shelter in the shade of its branches' (Ezek 17:23).

Jesus, however, described the kingdom as a mustard seed, proverbially the smallest of all seeds. The mustard seed is a parable of the kingdom's small beginnings. The people of Israel expected a mighty cedar, a Messiah who would come as a great king and leader, freeing Israel from Rome's oppressive rule and restoring the nation's former glory. Jesus made it clear, both in what he did and in his teachings, that the kingdom begins quietly and grows, often silently, upwards and outwards. It is always vulnerable, always risky, always bordering on the impossible, like a flower pushing its way up through a crack in the concrete.

The parable of the yeast, mixed (more accurately 'hidden') in a large amount of flour, carries the image further. For some reason, there is a secrecy about this action. The woman attempts to hide the yeast by putting it into far more flour than would normally be used. But of course the yeast refuses to stay hidden. It works its way, makes its presence known, and finally produces an enormous amount of leavened dough.

The mustard seed emphasises the small beginnings of the kingdom. The yeast emphasises the power of small beginnings to expand and eventually change the whole world.

What small beginnings or insignificant actions are you doing today in the name of Jesus? A random act of kindness, a lonely neighbour patiently listened to, an elderly person taken to a medical appointment, a meal delivered to someone recovering from surgery? Such things may seem just like a mustard seed or a spoonful of yeast, but so grows the kingdom!

To reflect on

Should we be concerned that thousands attend a rugby match, hundreds attend an orchestral performance, but only a handful of people turn up for a prayer meeting?

Surprises in the Kingdom

Luke 13:22–30

'Make every effort to enter through the narrow door, because many, I tell you, will try to enter and will not be able to' (v. 24, NIV).

If the beginnings are small but the result is great, will many be saved or just a few? So asks someone of Jesus as he makes his way to Jerusalem.

Jesus' answer is paradoxical. He warns his followers that many will come to the narrow door seeking entrance, only to be turned away. They will plead with the owner of the house that they have eaten with him and heard him teach. They know who he is. They have an acquaintanceship, a familiarity with him. But, Jesus says, this is not enough. He will send them away and admit others in their place.

Why will they be turned away? Have they come to the wrong door? Do they lack faith? Have they not done enough good works to qualify for entry? Jesus simply says, 'I do not know where you come from.' Yet others will come from east, west, north and south – anywhere and everywhere – and they will be admitted.

What makes us qualified for entrance into the kingdom of God? Knowing about Jesus is obviously not enough. Nor is familiarity with his teachings, doing good to one's neighbour, refraining from doing harm to one's neighbour, going to church (even twice!) on Sunday, keeping the rules, being bright or even brilliant, popular, wealthy or powerful. None of this is enough.

For all its mystery and ambiguity, this passage makes two things clear. Jesus encourages his followers to strive to enter by the narrow door, but he warns that, in the end, there will be many surprises in the kingdom. Many who think they will enter will not, and others who thought they would be excluded from God's fellowship will find themselves welcomed. Strive, says Jesus, as though admission to the kingdom depended entirely on your own doing, but know that ultimately it depends on God's grace.

To reflect on
One day we will find some in the kingdom of God whom we did not expect to find there. We will not find some whom we did expect to find there. The greatest surprise may be that we find ourselves there!

SUNDAY 10 APRIL
Weaving a Tapestry of Wisdom

Ecclesiastes 7:1–14

'When times are good, be happy; but when times are bad,
consider: God has made the one as well as the other' (v. 14, NIV).

These verses from Ecclesiastes hold seven sayings of wisdom that tell what is good for human beings. The words 'good' and 'better' weave like golden threads in a tapestry, in and out.

A good name is better than perfume, just as the day of death is better than the day of birth. The Old Testament is full of stories of people's efforts to make for themselves a good, or even a great name. The builders of the Tower of Babel tried to do that by building a city with a tower reaching to the heavens (*Gen 11:4*). In contrast, God offered to Abram and his descendants the very thing the tower builders could not do. 'I will make your name great, and you will be a blessing' (*Gen 12:2*).

Several sayings in this passage stress that a sober reflection on death is better than a foolish hilarity about living. 'A sad face is good for the heart' may not seem like good medical advice, but the Teacher is saying that a wise person should approach every experience of life with a keen sense of mortality, aware that death comes to everyone. The psalmist said, 'Teach us to number our days aright, that we may gain a heart of wisdom' (*Ps 90:12*). I read in the newspaper of a young man whose brother was killed in a tragic accident. Shock at his brother's accident and reflection on his own mortality jolted him out of his complacency and into a significant change of direction for his life.

The other sayings stress the importance of listening to criticism rather than effusive praise, the importance of finishing well what we begin and the foolishness of harking back to earlier times as 'the good old days'. Wisdom, the Teacher says, is like an inheritance, a good thing, a shelter and a life preserver. Life is a tangle of good times and bad, all made by God. If the day is good, be happy. If it is not, don't despair, for God is still in control, weaving his tapestry of life with both dark and glistening threads.

MONDAY 11 APRIL

Fox in the Hen House

Luke 13:31–35

'O Jerusalem, Jerusalem, you who kill the prophets and stone those sent to you, how often I have longed to gather your children together, as a hen gathers her chicks under her wings, but you were not willing!' (v. 34, NIV).

The Pharisees warn Jesus that Herod is out to kill him, but Jesus does not even flinch. 'I will drive out demons . . . I will reach my goal . . . I must keep going' (vv. 32,33). His mission is clear. He knows what he must do. With serenity Jesus moves towards Jerusalem, not to escape death but in order to embrace it.

From the beginning, Jesus has known the redemptive purposes of God being worked out in his life. 'I had to be in my Father's house,' he said when his anxious parents came looking for him (2:49). 'I must preach the good news of the kingdom of God to the other towns also,' he said when the crowd tried to make him stay (4:43). 'The Son of Man must suffer many things and be rejected . . . he must be killed and on the third day be raised to life' (9:22). 'Zacchaeus . . . I must stay at your house today,' he told the little man up the tree (19:5). ' "He was numbered with the transgressors" . . . this must be fulfilled in me' (22:37).

Where did such poise and purpose come from? Where does it come from for you and me? Surely in the daily listening, the daily walking, the daily staying close to the heart of God.

With great tenderness, Jesus addresses the people of Jerusalem. He knows he is going there to die. Jerusalem will reject him just as she has rejected and killed other prophets. The city will herself be devastated. She will not see Jesus again until he comes as the Son of Man. Jesus' words are fateful. Judgment hangs heavily in the air.

Two animal images symbolise the alternatives facing the people. Herod, the fox, represents the powerful who oppress God's people. Crafty and cunning, his methods are sneak and slaughter, devour and destroy. Pitted against him, Jesus is like a bird. Not an eagle with soaring wings and ripping talons, but a mother hen, vulnerable, flightless, defenceless, who can offer her young nothing more than the protective covering of her outstretched wings.

How will they choose?

TUESDAY 12 APRIL

Sick Man – Sabbath – Snare

Luke 14:1–6

'Jesus asked the Pharisees and experts in the law, "Is it lawful
to heal on the Sabbath or not?" ' (v. 3, NIV).

The setting for this healing miracle is a meal at the home of a prominent Pharisee. In any culture, eating is a significant social custom with certain norms of etiquette to be followed. As a rabbi, Jesus would be honoured, watched and listened to. But there is an undertone in this story suggesting that the careful watching is more than mere concern for an honoured guest's comfort. These religious leaders are out to trap Jesus, and he knows it.

Enter Exhibit A – a man suffering from dropsy, that is, the abnormal accumulation of fluids in the body. There is no reported dialogue with the man, no innocent-sounding questions from the Pharisees. But Jesus, who knows the heart and can read one's deepest thoughts, sums up the situation in just a moment. Sick man – Sabbath – Snare. Sounding innocent himself, he asks the question that goes to the very heart of the matter. 'Is it lawful to heal on the Sabbath or not?'

By asking the question before he actually performs the miracle, Jesus forces the onlookers to respond. If they say, 'No, it is not lawful to heal on the Sabbath,' they will be revealing their own lack of compassion. If they say, 'Yes, it is lawful,' they will be going against their own tradition with its multitudinous interpretations. Either way, they are caught in a trap of their own making.

They remain silent. Jesus heals the man and sends him off. Then he turns to the Pharisees with another question. 'Is there anyone here who, if a child or animal fell down a well, wouldn't rush to pull him out immediately, not asking whether or not it was the Sabbath?' (v. 5, *The Message*).

Again they have nothing to say. A response would only dig them in deeper. Their silence concedes Jesus the victory. Human need takes precedence over Sabbath observance. This healing shows that the religious leaders still do not get the point of Jesus' ministry. Sin is blinding. A hard heart is tough to break. There are none so deaf as those who have no desire to hear.

WEDNESDAY 13 APRIL
Honour and Hospitality

Luke 14:7–14

'Everyone who exalts himself will be humbled, and he who humbles himself will be exalted' (v. 11, NIV).

In Luke's Gospel Jesus is often on his way to a meal, at a meal or coming from a meal. Luke tells us where he ate (5:29), and with whom (5:30), whether he washed before eating (11:38) and the normal customs of hospitality before a meal (7:44–46).

A meal table was usually in the shape of a U and the host sat at the base. The seats of honour were located next to him. The company one kept and the place one had at table said a great deal about one's social standing. Jesus takes the opportunity of a meal at the house of a prominent Pharisee to make a few strong statements about honour and hospitality. He speaks first to the guests and then to the host.

Noticing that the guests are choosing for themselves the place of honour, Jesus tells them to save themselves embarrassment by not choosing the best seat, and to guarantee themselves honour by actually choosing, not just a lower place, but the lowest place. We hear an echo of his words that the first will be last and the last first (13:30).

This is more than a lesson in honour and shame at the meal table. Jesus is speaking a kingdom principle. While the world considers honour to be the first place, top dog, number one, in the kingdom of God the path to honour is by way of humility, the towel and basin, the downward bend of service. One's true worth is to be found, not in the recognition of one's peers, but in the certainty of God's acceptance.

Jesus' words to his host make a similar point. He lists four groups that one should not invite to a meal – friends, brothers and sisters, relatives, or rich neighbours – simply because these ones are able to return the invitation. Choose instead, he says, the poor, the crippled, the lame, the blind – those who have no chance of repaying. God, who does not look on the glitter of our guest list but on the openness of our heart, will reward us with his blessing.

THURSDAY 14 APRIL

Excuses! Excuses!

Luke 14:15–24

'At the time of the banquet he sent his servant to tell those who had been invited, "Come, for everything is now ready" ' (v. 17, NIV).

A man sitting at the table listening to Jesus makes a comment about the blessedness of those who will sit at the banquet table in the kingdom. He may be trying to ease the tension that Jesus' remarks have caused. 'When we all get to heaven, won't that be wonderful,' he is saying.

Jesus responds with a story of 'a certain man' who prepares a great banquet and invites many guests. The host is obviously a wealthy man of high social standing. When everything is ready, he sends his servant to tell the invited guests to come.

One by one, they politely decline the invitation which they had previously accepted. 'I have just bought some land. I must go and see it.' 'I have just bought some oxen. I must go and try them out.' 'I have just got married. I cannot come.' The first two excuses are patently absurd. No one would buy land without inspecting it first. No one would buy farm equipment without first trying it out.

The third excuse is a flat refusal to come. 'The little woman won't let me,' or maybe, 'I'm still recovering from the cost of getting married and I cannot afford another social debt at the moment.'

When the host hears these excuses masquerading as reasons, he is justifiably angry. He has been insulted but he turns the insult back on the initially invited guests. He tells his servant to go and bring in the poor, the crippled, the blind and lame to fill up the vacant places. When there is still room for more, he sends the servant out again, this time to bring in the outcasts, the homeless, the landless. Finally every seat at the banquet is filled with those who have no voice, no rights, no social standing. There is no chance of any place being left for those who were first invited. The first have indeed become last and the last first.

The kingdom invitation is offered to all. The only reason for not coming in is one's own deliberate choice.

What's your excuse? Watch your excuse!

FRIDAY 15 APRIL
Costly Discipleship

Luke 14:25–33

'If anyone comes to me and does not hate his father and mother, his wife and children, his brothers and sisters – yes, even his own life – he cannot be my disciple' (v. 26, NIV).

The meal is over; the journey towards Jerusalem resumes. Jesus speaks some deep and serious matters both to his disciples and to the large crowds who travel with him.

Knowing that death awaits him in Jerusalem, he urges those who want to be his disciples to consider carefully what such a commitment means. 'Anyone who does not . . . cannot be my disciple' (v. 27). Jesus cannot be accused of tempting his followers with a soft gospel, cheap grace, an easy road. He lays down three conditions for discipleship.

The first has to do with family ties. Jesus uses the word 'hate', but it is to be understood as a comparative word, not as an expression of hostility or anger. Jesus is saying that if there is a conflict of interest, a choice to be made between Jesus or family, one's response to the demands of discipleship must take precedence over even the most sacred of human relationships.

The second condition has to do with cross-bearing. This is not wearing a cross around one's neck as a fashion statement, nor even complaining of a stubborn husband as 'the cross God has given me to bear'. Carrying one's cross means facing the same fate as Jesus did – rejection, suffering, loneliness – as one consistently lives out the values of the kingdom.

He tells two parables to illustrate his point. No one lays a foundation for a tower unless he is sure he can finish building it. No military leader goes to war unless he is sure he has enough soldiers to defeat the enemy. The parables are not about building smaller towers or bigger armies, but about counting the cost of discipleship and being sure one can see the project through.

The third condition for discipleship has to do with forsaking possessions, giving up (literally 'saying farewell to') everything for the sake of the gospel. Jesus speaks the hard realities of discipleship. 'Do you love me?' he asked Peter (*John 21:17*). 'How much?' he asks you and me today.

To reflect on
Jesus calls us not just to a decision, but to a relationship.

SATURDAY 16 APRIL
A Salty Christian

Luke 14:34–35

'Salt is good, but if it loses its saltiness, how can it be made salty again?' (v. 34, NIV).

These verses on salt come at the end of a rather sober passage about the cost of discipleship. At first glance the image does not seem to fit, until we consider what salt is for.

The value of salt lies in its saltiness. Real salt cannot lose its flavour, but the complex minerals around the Dead Sea were not pure salt and could, therefore, become tasteless. Once lost, the taste could not be restored. Jesus comments that salt that has lost its taste is not even good for garden fertiliser or for killing weeds. In other words, such salt is not even good for menial, alternative uses. 'It's useless, good for nothing' (v. 35, *The Message*). It might as well be thrown out (*Matt 5:13*).

Salt is used for flavouring and preserving food. Without salt, food is flavourless. With salt, the natural flavours of the food may be heightened. A bucketful is not needed, just a dusting, just a pinch. Salt is used for cleaning and disinfecting. I remember as a child having to soak my foot in a bowl of hot salty water after a minor operation.

Jesus displays his skill once again at using familiar everyday objects such as water, bread, seeds, light, fire, and now salt to explain the truths of the kingdom. The parallels between salt and discipleship are clear.

A salty Christian is one who has a personal relationship with Jesus. A salty Christian has a distinctive 'flavour', a consistent, godly, reliable attitude that others can depend on. A salty Christian has a cleansing, purifying effect on those around him. Notice how foul language in the workplace often changes when someone declares himself to be a Christian. A salty Christian seeks to live peaceably with others (see *Mark 9:50*). A salty Christian makes others thirsty for their own close relationship with God.

To reflect on

Let Jesus' words take you to the kitchen cupboard today. Put a pinch of salt on your hand, then on your tongue, and ask yourself the question, 'When it comes to flavouring, preserving and cleansing, how salty am I?'

SUNDAY 17 APRIL
A Song of Opportunity

Ecclesiastes 11:1–6

'Sow your seed in the morning, and at evening let not your hands
be idle, for you do not know which will succeed, whether this or that,
or whether both will do equally well' (v. 6, NIV).

In Spenser's *Faerie Queene*, Opportunity is personified as a woman whose long hair flows out in front of her, but the back of her head is bald. What this means is that Opportunity can be grabbed only from the front. Once she is past, it is too late.

These verses from Ecclesiastes remind us that life is a mixture of opportunity and risk. The writer encourages us to be generous and open-handed in our living. Giving portions to seven or eight sounds like a lot of extras at the meal table when you are perhaps used to serving up for just one or two. Sending out bread upon the waters sounds wasteful. Surely it will just become soggy, no good for anything but duck food. If bread here is to be understood as ships being sent away, laden with cargo, that too seems risky. What guarantee is there that they will reach their destination? Will they return empty or laden with treasure? Will they return at all?

The writer of Ecclesiastes is not unlike Jesus, who told the story of the sower broadcasting his seed near and far. The sower seemed unconcerned about the stony path, the narrow shelf of soil, the thorn bushes or the ever-watchful hungry birds. Confident of a harvest, he flung his seed out widely and wildly.

It takes courage to live like this, of course. It takes courage for someone to work among Aids sufferers in the suburbs of Lusaka. It takes courage for a nurse to live among the rubble of Baghdad or beside rubbish heaps in the Philippines. It takes courage to light a candle to illumine someone else's darkness.

Living cautiously, always playing it safe, has consequences as well. Live like this and you may be paralysed into inaction. Watch the weather and your crops may waste. If you wait for perfect conditions, whether to plant a tree, to begin a course of study or to take steps to grow spiritually, you will never get anything done.

To reflect on
Today, if you see Opportunity coming, grab her while you can!

MONDAY 18 APRIL

A Chapter of Losts and Founds

Luke 15:1–2

'Now the tax collectors and "sinners" were all gathering around to hear him' (v. 1, NIV).

This chapter of Luke's Gospel contains three stories of lost and found things – a sheep, a coin and a son. They are all precious – the sheep to the shepherd, the coin to the woman, the son to his father. The stories need to be read together for they are bound with common themes of lostness, recovery and rejoicing.

The trigger for the stories is a murmuring from the Pharisees and teachers of the law against Jesus. 'This man welcomes sinners, and eats with them' (v. 2), they say. 'Watch your company at table, as far as you are able' is one of their theme songs. The tax collectors, prostitutes and other such 'unclean ones' with whom they see Jesus keeping company are, according to the Pharisees, generally categorised as 'sinners'. They are to be avoided at all costs, kept at arm's length or even further, if at all possible. But Jesus sees these people as lost ones who need to be found.

What is it with these Pharisees? They are good men, holy men, righteous men. They speak religious language and do fine acts of piety, yet so often their ways of seeing are diametrically opposed to Jesus' way. They follow religion to the finest point, yet seem to have no desire for a relationship with God. They are familiar with every religious principle yet know nothing of the Person. They speak tradition but not testimony. They observe the incarnate Son of God and watch the kingdom of God being lived out in what he does, but it is as if they cannot see, cannot hear, cannot comprehend what stands right in front of them.

In response to the Pharisees' grumbling Jesus tells these three stories. They should be read with care for they are more than just pretty parables. They contain challenges that pull us right in and demand that we too make a response, both to the God who searches and to those whom we know to be lost. The whole gospel and its call to mission is written here between the lines of these three stories.

TUESDAY 19 APRIL
One of a Hundred

Luke 15:3–7

'Suppose one of you has a hundred sheep and loses one of them'
(v. 4, NIV).

The first story tells of a shepherd and his flock of one hundred sheep. He may be the owner of the sheep, or he may be employed by the owner to care for them. As the shepherd counts the sheep at the end of the day he comes up one short. He counts again but is still one short.

Leaving the other ninety-nine, he goes searching for the lost one. Anxiously he scans the horizon and looks up onto the rocky crags near to where the sheep have been grazing. He cannot see anything unusual. He cannot hear the bleating of a sheep caught in a thorn bush. But he knows that thorn bushes are not a sheep's worst enemies. There are hungry wolves among the crags, hiding in the shade and in the cleft of the rocks.

As he searches he calls out the name of the lost sheep. He sings his distinctive high-pitched song that the sheep would recognise. This man, skilled in the ways of sheep, stars and signs, notices a track heading away from where the flock had been grazing during the day. A short dip into a hidden valley brings him upon the lost sheep, its foot caught in a hole. With tender hands the shepherd releases the bruised hoof, picks up the sheep and carries it back to the sheepfold. Delighted at finding this lost one alive and well, the shepherd calls to his friends. They too know the anxiety of losing a sheep and the joy of finding it again. Together they celebrate.

This is a picture of the Shepherd God (see *Ps 23:1*) who seeks those who are lost. This is the Shepherd God who 'gathers the lambs in his arms and carries them close to his heart' (*Isa 40:11*). Such a glad finding is the cue for the angels in heaven to rejoice. Is this your 'lost and found' story today?

He sought me, he sought me,
When I was wandering far away;
He found me, he found me,
O what a wonderful day!
Sidney Cox, SASB 386

WEDNESDAY 20 APRIL

One of Ten

Luke 15:8–10

'Suppose a woman has ten silver coins and loses one' (v. 8, NIV).

From one of a hundred to one of ten, this next parable tells of a woman searching for a lost coin. Two possibilities paint the backdrop to this story. It could be that the lost coin is one of ten silver coins that she, as a Palestinian woman, received on her wedding day. As well as its monetary value, such a coin would have great sentimental value. To lose one would be very distressing indeed.

Or it could be that this is just a small coin of limited value, about a day's wages, that's all. If the woman is poor, maybe a widow, then even the smallest coin will be precious and she will search carefully before writing it off as permanently lost.

The parable paints a picture of a woman focused on her search. This is her task, her priority. Everything else can wait for the moment. Her house, typical of the time, will have a dirt floor, a small door and no window. Searching for a lost coin will be difficult, but she lights a lamp, sweeps the house and searches carefully. She may find other lost items as she works her way methodically from wall to wall, but her search is for one thing – her lost coin. When at last she finds it, she calls together her friends and neighbours and tells the story of her glad finding.

In both this and the previous parable, the emphasis is on rejoicing at the recovery of that which was lost. How do the Pharisees and teachers of the law hear these stories? Do they realise they are being put under the spotlight?

These parables also pose some penetrating questions to you and me as we read them. Do you rejoice when others rejoice, weep when they weep? How do you respond when God's blessing is poured out on someone else? Do you judge others by merit ('They deserved that!') or by mercy ('Thank you, God, for being good to them')? A woman with a lamp, a broom and a large smile on her face puts these questions to us today.

THURSDAY 21 APRIL

One of Two

Luke 15:11–20a

'There was a man who had two sons' (v. 11, NIV).

Take one son – tousled-haired, adventurous. Watch him approach his father – disrespectful, demanding. 'Dad, I can't wait until you are dead' – insulting, offensive. 'Give me my inheritance now' – impatient, rebellious. See him pack his belongings – careless, carefree. Follow his tracks as he heads off to a far place – unknown, pagan. See how he lives – irresponsible, loose. Watch him squander his fortune – dissolute, reckless.

Feel the famine squeeze the country – needy, tight. See him pleading for work – desperate, hungry. Watch him feeding pigs – humiliated, degraded. Notice the scraps he feeds on – slushy, disgusting. Observe a gradual change – thoughtful, remembering. Hear his plan – decisive, determined. Listen to his speech – repentant, humble. Watch him head home – trudging, weary.

Who is this boy with no name? Call him prodigal, label him lost. Colour his world with splashes of selfishness and smears of rebellion. Fill the air with the sound of scoffing and the smell of pig slops. Blister his feet with the endless journey back home.

This dissolute-living boy is a picture of every child who turns away from the father, then repents and returns. He heads home physically exhausted, mentally spent, emotionally wasted, spiritually bankrupt. He comes wearing the rags of a riotous life turned mouldy, pushed homeward by the hunger pains in his stomach, and a speech churning around in his head.

This prodigal son is you or me. We may not be young, tousle-haired or rebellious. We may never have demanded our inheritance or gone off and squandered our lives in a far country. We may never have felt hunger pangs or humiliation. We may never have hit rock bottom before we came to our senses and headed back home again. But there is something in this boy's attitude that is uncomfortably familiar. Change the backdrop, put you and me on stage, and we too own a story something like this, punctuated with demand, grab and run.

---

*Afar from Heaven thy feet have
  wandered,
Afar from God thy soul has strayed;
His gifts in sin thy hand has
  squandered,
Yet still in love he calls thee home.*
                    Richard Slater, SASB 225

FRIDAY 22 APRIL
The Forgiving Father

Luke 15:20b–24

'While he was still a long way off, his father saw him and was filled with compassion for him; he ran to his son, threw his arms around him and kissed him' (v. 20b, NIV).

With a bag full of broken dreams, a young man heads home. With a heart full of compassion, a father waits for his return.

At the start of the story, this father gave the boy what he demanded – generous, open-handed. He knows that love which forces and controls is not love at all – wise, understanding. He watches the boy leave – heartbroken, sorrowful. He strains to hear news from a far country – listening, praying. Every morning he scans the horizon – watching, longing. Every noontime and evening he does it again – waiting, hoping.

One day he sees a lone figure in the distance – staggering, stumbling. The old man's heart leaps – hopeful, breathless. He gathers up his robes and runs – ridiculous, undignified. As he gets near the boy he recognises him – overjoyed, excited. He throws his arms around his son's thin frame – overwhelmed, grateful. He scarcely hears the boy's muffled speech – welcoming, weeping.

He leads the boy home – joyful, amazed. He orders a robe to be thrown over the boy's shoulders, a ring to be placed on his finger, new shoes on his feet – extravagant, hospitable. He signals for the fattened calf to be slaughtered, a party to be prepared – rejoicing, celebrating. He calls his neighbours and friends to come – restoring, reconciling.

Who is this father full of forgiveness, mantled in mercy, who so lavishly and so joyfully welcomes his returning son? This is a picture of God the Father who throws a party every time a sinner turns back home again. This is the God who, throughout the Scriptures, is described as 'compassionate and gracious, slow to anger, abounding in love' (Ps 103:8). This is the God who 'does not treat us as our sins deserve or repay us according to our iniquities' (Ps 103:10). This is the God who stands at the edge of your village and mine, waiting for the first sign of our return home.

O Jesus, full of truth and grace,
More full of grace than I of sin,
Yet once again I seek thy face,
Open thine arms and take me in.
Charles Wesley, SASB 305

SATURDAY 23 APRIL
The Begrudging Brother

Luke 15:25-32

'Meanwhile the older son was in the field. When he came near
the house, he heard music and dancing' (v. 25, NIV).

Out in the fields, another brother is just finishing his day's work – dutiful, responsible. Today is no different from any other – routine, predictable. As he approaches the house he hears music – noisy, partying. He hears the sounds of rejoicing – exuberant, excited. He asks what it all means – puzzling, questioning. He is told his brother has returned – battered, repentant. His father has welcomed him with open arms – forgiving, restoring. The older brother refuses to go in and join the party – begrudging, annoyed. He knows what he would give his brother – punishing, judging. He hears what his father has given – amazing, extravagant.

When his father comes out to plead with him, he feels angry and annoyed. 'Look,' he says – put out, furious. 'All these years I've been slaving for you' – self-righteous, proud. 'You never gave me' – bitter, resentful. 'But this son of yours' – seething, suspicious. 'My son,' the father pleads – merciful, compassionate. 'You are always with me and everything I have is yours' – open-handed, generous. 'Your brother was dead and is alive again' – lost, found. 'Won't you come in and join the celebrations?' – appealing, pleading.

Who is this brother standing back in the shadows, watching, uninvolved? He represents the attitude of the Pharisees who observed and criticised Jesus for the way in which he spoke to, dined with, and embraced sinners. At the start of this chapter, the Pharisees are recorded as saying, 'This man welcomes sinners and eats with them.' The story Jesus tells is his way of saying, 'You think that is bad? Hey, I not only eat with sinners, I run down the road when I see them coming, I fling my arms around them and welcome them home!'

In telling this greatest 'lost and found' story of all time, Jesus puts the Pharisees on the spot. Will they be like the father, forgiving and compassionate, or will they continue to be self-righteous and resentful at what God is doing? The story ends with the question hanging in the air. Does the older brother go in and join the party? Do the Pharisees change their tune? What would you do?

119

SUNDAY 24 APRIL

Life is a Fleeting Breath

Ecclesiastes 11:7–12:8

'Remember your Creator in the days of your youth, before the days of trouble come and the years approach when you will say, "I find no pleasure in them" ' (12:1, NIV).

The book of Ecclesiastes begins with the haunting refrain, ' "Meaningless! Meaningless!" says the Teacher. "Utterly meaningless! Everything is meaningless" ' (1:2). We also know it as, 'Vanity of vanities! All is vanity!'

As the book begins, so it ends, with the refrain repeated (12:8). It is easy to write this document off as the pessimistic ponderings of a discouraged old man. He has lived a long life, has seen it all, and has come to the bleak conclusion that nothing makes any ultimate sense. A close reading of the book, however, shows that between his opening and closing declarations there is a call to live life to the full. Why? Not because life has no meaning or purpose, but because it is short and fleeting.

The Teacher addresses his words to a young man, urging him to rejoice during the time of light, but to remember that the darkness is coming. The first seven verses of Chapter 12 are all one sentence in the Hebrew. To get the best dramatic effect from this passage, read the verses out loud in the style of a clock running down. These verses

are a picture of ageing. One day the light will fade, the strong men (shoulders) will stoop, the grinders (teeth) will cease, those looking through the windows (eyes) will grow dim, the sound of birds will grow faint, the life force will fail and death will surely come.

'Remember!' says the Teacher. Keep this end in focus but, in the meantime, there is much to experience – enjoying the sound of birds and the taste of food, savouring intimacy and love, living fully into life. While we have time there is work to do – loving and raising children, building friendships and memories, writing poems and sermons, performing music and miracles, creating delicious meals and works of art.

These things must be done before the precious water of life is poured out, the dust returns to the ground, and the spirit of a person returns to God who gave it. Life is a fleeting breath. Draw deeply, live fully, love extravagantly.

MONDAY 25 APRIL
A Shrewd Manager

Luke 16:1–9

'There was a rich man whose manager was accused of wasting his possessions' (v. 1, NIV).

This puzzling story features two people – a rich man, who may have been an absentee landlord, and his steward, the manager of his property. The rich man is informed that his steward has been wasting ('squandering', NRSV) his possessions. This is exactly what the prodigal son did far from home (15:13). The rich man tells the steward his job is on the line and orders him to prepare an audit of his transactions.

Facing a future with no job and no income, the steward considers his options. He is not strong enough to do manual labour and is too proud to beg. He hits on a plan to use the resources he has at hand, namely his master's debtors. He takes an inventory of the debts owing and, one by one, reduces the amounts.

The first debt is for eight hundred gallons of olive oil. This is a huge amount, worth about three years' salary. The steward reduces it to four hundred gallons. He does something similar with the next debt, rewriting a thousand bushels of wheat as eight hundred.

What is not made clear in the parable is the reasoning of the steward. By reducing the amounts owed, is he simply being dishonest to his master? Or is he cutting out his own commission, thereby taking the loss himself? Or is he reducing an inflated charge that his master made as a way of getting round the Mosaic prohibition against charging interest to one's fellow Jews (see Deut 23:19)?

Whatever lies behind the steward's actions, everyone comes out a winner. The steward has cast an aura of honesty and generosity on his master, delighted the master's debtors, and shrewdly provided for his own future. The debtors are now honour–bound to act with benevolence towards him.

What is this story saying about the gospel? 'What is that in your hand?' God asked Moses (Exod 4:2), when he was commissioning him to rescue the Israelites from Egypt. Perhaps he asks the same thing of us today. Are we using carefully, both for today and for tomorrow, what God has entrusted to us?

TUESDAY 26 APRIL

Faithful with Little . . . Entrusted with Much

Luke 16:10–12

'Whoever can be trusted with very little can also be trusted with much, and whoever is dishonest with very little will also be dishonest with much' (v. 10, NIV).

In Jewish folklore the story is told of a man who was sentenced to death for stealing some bread. He told his guard it was a pity he was going to die as he had a wonderful secret the king really needed to hear. He said he knew how to plant a pomegranate seed that would grow overnight and bear fruit the very next day.

The guard reported this to the king, who was curious and asked to see the man. With the king and his guard watching, the man dug a hole, then said, 'In order for this to work, the seed must be planted by someone who has never stolen. I stole some bread so I cannot plant it.'

His guard admitted that, in his younger days, he had kept something that did not belong to him. Then the king confessed that he had once taken something from his father. The man said, 'You are both powerful men. You want for nothing. Yet you cannot plant the seed because of your dishonesty, while I, who stole some bread because I was starving, am now to be hanged.' The king, recognising the man's shrewdness, pardoned him.

In Jesus' parable (vv. 1–8), the steward does something similar. He acts decisively and shrewdly to provide for his own future. Jesus uses the story as a launching pad for some strong words about faithfulness and integrity, qualities that are often shown in how one manages money and possessions. Jesus' principles are just as true for us as they were for his first audience.

Jesus is saying that, if you know how to spend a small amount carefully, you will know how to handle a large amount. But if you are dishonest or foolish with a small amount, you will certainly not be able to handle a large amount. If you are not trustworthy with what you have been given to care for on earth, you will be unfit to handle the vast riches of God's kingdom.

To reflect on
Many tests of integrity track a path from the heart right to the wallet.

WEDNESDAY 27 APRIL
An Undivided Heart

Luke 16:13–15

'He said to them, "You are the ones who justify yourselves in the eyes of men, but God knows your hearts" ' (v. 15, NIV).

Jesus speaks about integrity and faithfulness, but the religious leaders sneer at him. Like a two-edged sword, his words cut deep, close to the bone. He tells them it is impossible to serve two masters. The inevitable result is hating one and loving the other.

The Pharisees were religious people who professed their love for God by following God's command-ments and keeping the law, as well as a multitude of their own inter-pretations. But Luke describes them as people 'who loved money'. They obviously see no conflict in the matter. They consider their wealth to be evidence of God's blessing. They love the power, the position, the prestige that money gives them.

But God, who sees and knows all things, knows that the heart cannot be divided. 'You have to choose one or the other,' Jesus says. 'You cannot profess to have faith in God and put your confidence in your wealth at the same time. Two such all-absorbing passions cannot live together equally.'

Not only in the Gospels, but throughout the Scriptures, a call to having a pure, single-focused heart is sounded. 'Love the Lord your God with all your heart,' God told the children of Israel (*Deut 6:5*). 'Give me an undivided heart,' begged the psalmist (*Ps 86:11*). 'Above all else, guard your heart,' said the writer of Proverbs (*Prov 4:23*). The state of one's heart determines how one lives and speaks (*Luke 6:45*). Where one's treasure is determines where one's heart will be (*12:34*). People can be deceived, but there is no way to deceive God. He alone knows what is in every person's heart.

Jesus' words have a sobering effect on the Pharisees, for the moment at least. They sneer at him but they know – in their hearts – that he speaks truth. In just a short time they will seek to silence the message by slaughtering the messenger.

O for a heart whiter than snow!
Saviour Divine, to whom else shall I
*   go?*
Thou who didst die, loving me so,
Give me a heart that is whiter than
*   snow.*

Eliza Hewitt, SASB 443

THURSDAY 28 APRIL
The New Era of God's Kingdom

Luke 16:16–18

'The Law and the Prophets were proclaimed until John. Since that time, the good news of the kingdom of God is being preached' (v. 16, NIV).

These verses of 'Additional Teachings', as they are headed up in some Bibles, seem out of place here, sandwiched between the parable of the shrewd manager and the story of the rich man and Lazarus. Yet the verses complement the themes of integrity and faithfulness that sound throughout this chapter.

The first two verses of today's reading are like a hinge. Until the time of John the Baptist, God's ways and words were made known to people by the law and the prophets. Through a long series of spokesmen, God made clear his commandments and principles for godly living.

With the coming of Jesus, however, the *Logos*, the Word of God, arrived in person (see *John 1:14*), ushering in a new era. As Jesus preached the kingdom, people saw and understood the good news, not just as principles to live by, but as a relationship to live in. A movement took place. What had once been written on tablets of stone was now written onto human hearts, just as God said would happen (see *Jer 31:31–34; Heb 8:6–12*). The old order

of things was sealed with the blood of sacrificial animals. The new order is sealed by the blood of Christ poured out once and for all.

John the Baptist's ministry was thus a dividing line between the Old and New Testaments (see *John 1:15*). Jesus' ministry and teaching did not cancel out what God had said through the prophets but, rather, brought it all to fulfilment. Everything in the Old Testament pointed towards Jesus. When he came, bringing in the kingdom of God, every Old Testament promise was fulfilled.

It is against this background, and in the context of this chapter's teaching on integrity and faithfulness, that we read the verse on divorce and adultery. In a society where divorce had become as easy as a few set words being said and a certificate of divorce being issued, Jesus restates in stark terms the standard that God set down right at the beginning of time (see *Gen 2:24*), namely that marriage is to be a permanent, lifetime commitment.

FRIDAY 29 APRIL
Death – the Great Leveller

Luke 16:19–22

'The time came when the beggar died and the angels carried him to Abraham's side. The rich man also died and was buried' (v. 22, NIV).

In case Jesus' strong words about money are not enough, he tells a story, a drama in three acts, that challenges many of the Pharisees' cosy beliefs about wealth and possessions.

In the first act, the rich are rich and the poor are poor. The two main characters are described but there is no conversation or inter-action between them. Their lives are separated by a table, a gate and a vast chasm of social status.

The rich man is not named. He could be any rich individual. He wears purple, which suggests he may be a high-ranking official or even royalty. His fine linen is a description of the quality of his undergarments. He lives in a house with a gate that gives him privacy and security and separates him from the riff-raff of the city. He feasts sumptuously every day. He has everything he could ever want.

At the rich man's gate is laid (literally 'thrown') a poor crippled beggar whose body is covered with running sores. His name, Lazarus, comes from Eleazar, meaning 'God helps'. Sadly, no one else helps Lazarus. He would be content to eat the soiled bread from the rich man's table, that is, the bread used to wipe the grease from one's hands. The dogs of the street, who probably get those scraps to eat, lick the beggar's sores, thus making him ceremonially unclean. His situation is as tragic as the rich man's is sumptuous.

In the second act of the drama, the rich become poor and the poor become rich. What is set up in the first part of the story is now reversed.

Lazarus dies of starvation and disease and is carried by the angels to Abraham's side (literally 'bosom'), the place of blessedness, comfort and consolation. In life he was neglected by others, but in death he is highly valued in the sight of God (see v. 15). Unexpectedly, the rich man also dies. Perhaps he dies of overeating, while Lazarus starves to death. There are no angels for this rich man. He is simply 'buried', probably in a beautiful purple shroud.

SATURDAY 30 APRIL

An Open-ended Story

Luke 16:23–31

'If they do not listen to Moses and the Prophets, they will not be convinced even if someone rises from the dead' (v. 31, NIV).

In the third act of Jesus' story, the poor are rich and the rich are poor. The rich man calls 'Father Abraham' to send Lazarus to dip his finger in the water to cool his tongue. The rich man knows Lazarus's name and presumably knew of his plight as he lay starving at the gate, yet he did nothing to help him at that time. 'Send Lazarus,' he begs. He obviously still sees the poor man as beneath him in status and therefore able to be his servant.

Lazarus, who never asked for anything on earth, still says nothing, but Abraham speaks for him. 'Remember . . .' he says (v. 25). The chasm of social status and indifference that separated Lazarus from the rich man in life is now an impassable chasm that prevents Lazarus from responding with compassion to the rich man's torment. So the rich man begs Abraham to send Lazarus on another errand – back to warn his five brothers. If there is no hope for him, at least he may be able to intervene and spare them from this same torment.

But, Abraham responds, they know what Moses and the prophets (that is, the Old Testament Scriptures) say about being merciful and treating the poor with compassion. 'Let them listen to them.' 'No, that won't be enough,' wails the rich man. 'It will take far more than that for them to repent.'

Using Abraham as his spokesman, Jesus gives the punchline to the story. If they (that is, the Pharisees or anyone) will not listen to and live out the commandments, then even a resurrection (his own) will not be enough to change their hard-heartedness.

Like the story of the prodigal son, this one is open-ended and invites us right in. Are you a rich man, unconcerned about the people at your 'gate'? Are you a Lazarus, relying daily on the mercy and gracious help of God? Or are you one of the rich man's five anonymous brothers, still needing to make a decision about repentance and faith?

We each must write our own ending to this story.

NOTES

1   'Pilgrimage' by Joy Cowley, taken from *Psalms for the Road*, published by and copyright © Catholic Supplies (NZ) Ltd, PO Box 16–110, Wellington, New Zealand; email: catholic.supplies@clear.net.nz.

2   Henri Nouwen, *The Inner Voice of Love: A Journey through Anguish to Freedom*, Darton, Longman & Todd, 1997.

3   Jane Grayshon, *A Pathway to Pain*; revised editon: Monarch Books, 2002.

4   J. R. R. Tolkien, *The Return of the King*, latest edition: HarperCollins, 2003.

5   Diane Ball, 'In His Time', copyright ©1978 CCIM Music/Maranatha! Music and administered by CopyCare, PO Box 77, Hailsham, East Sussex BN27 3EF, music@copycare.com. Used by permission.

6   Henri Nouwen, *The Inner Voice of Love: A Journey through Anguish to Freedom*, Darton, Longman & Todd, 1997.

INDEX

(as from Advent 1999)

Words of Life Bible reading notes
are published three times a year:

Easter
(January–April)

Pentecost
(May–August)

Advent
(September–December)

In each edition you will find:

- informative commentary
- a wide variety of Bible passages
- topics for praise and prayer
- points to ponder
- cross references for further study

Why not place a regular order for *Words of Life*?
Collect each volume and build a lasting resource
for personal or group study. If you require further
information about how you can receive copies of
Words of Life, please contact: The Literary Secretary,
101 Queen Victoria Street, London EC4P 4EP, England.
Alternatively, telephone (020) 7332 8065 or
e-mail IHQ-Editorial@salvationarmy.org

If you would like to contact Barbara Sampson,
her e-mail address is:

barbara_sampson@nzf.salvationarmy.org